Thoughts About *The Expert's Edge*

Brilliance is defined as "distilling the complex...to the simple," which is just what Ken Lizotte has accomplished. Ken's latest work is a must read for CEOs who want a practical way to separate themselves and their companies from their competitors. I'm putting it at the top of my recommended CEO reading list.

FRED W. GREEN
Chairman of the Chief Executive Officers' Club of Boston

Ken Lizotte has brought thought leadership to a science and an art—and on the road to becoming a mainstream term.

LOUIS CARTER
CEO, Best Practice Institute

The Expert's Edge should be required reading on every manager's and executive's bookshelf. By practicing what author Ken Lizotte calls "thoughtleading actions," your competition will fade away. Take a good look at this book ... then do what it says!

FLORENCE STONE
Editorial Director, American Management Association

The Expert's Edge, through Mr. Lizotte's "thoughtleading" strategy, provides a formidable and adaptable arsenal of skills to ensure personal success. It is particularly suited to the ongoing and evolving challenge of what encompasses work and career in today's world. I certainly can recommend it to our students, my colleagues, and any professional. Read it! You will find yourself starting to think differently, and more successfully, after only a few chapters.

LYNN RUBLEE
Academic Advisor, Harvard University Extension School

Forget all you have heard about "classic marketing." Become a thought-leader and you will reach audiences as you have never done before.

DRUMM MCNAUGHTON, PH.D., CMC®
Chair-President, The Change Leader, Inc.
and Chair-Elect, Institute of Management Consultants USA

If you're aspiring to be a thoughtleader in your field, you couldn't find a better guidebook than Ken Lizotte's *The Expert's Edge*. It's a no-frills, cut-to-the-chase manual for mastering the tools of visionary leadership in a fast-paced, ever-changing world.

JAN PHILLIPS
Author of *The Art of Original Thinking:*
The Making of a Thought Leader

There is an old expression that says that knowledge is power. Yet, if no one knows you have the knowledge, does it matter? Ken Lizotte, with his concept of being a thoughtleader, helps experts create market visibility that they could never achieve on their own. He also helps experts come out of the shadows and into the limelight. Having knowledge is one thing. Being recognized as an expert is another. The knowledge-able starve while the thoughtleaders thrive!

LEE B. SALZ
Author of *Soar Despite Your Dodo Sales Manager*
and President of Sales Dodo

Want to be the leader in your field? Read this book. Highlight important passages. Make notes in the margin on how you will apply its many valuable ideas. Read it now. Reread it in 18 months. Keep it on your desk. Refer to it often. You can't be seen as an expert without it.

SEAN GALLAGHER
Chief Value Delivery Officer, MarketCulture Strategies

To my best girls, all three of them

Contents

Forethought

What Is the Expert's Edge?

Beware when the great God lets loose a thinker on this planet.

RALPH WALDO EMERSON

WHENEVER ENTREPRENEURS of any kind gather, the first question of consequence to emerge in their conversations is always this one: "How do you find new business?"

It might be phrased like this:

- "How do you find your customers?"
- "How do people hear about you?"
- "How do you market your services?"
- "How do you generate leads?"

Typically, the responses revolve around some variation of referrals and word of mouth, and the focus invariably shifts to marketing, selling, "outreach," or business development techniques. The conversation falls flat once someone mentions cold calling (a technique that everyone agrees is disagreeable!), then collapses altogether once direct mail or advertising gets dropped in.

From there, talk turns to idle chatter, personal questions, the weather—anything to push the topic at hand away from its disappointing beginnings. There are no business development magic bullets or gold nuggets here. Why bother beating a dead horse?

Entrepreneurs today are exasperated. There's so much competition, so many new technologies to use (and learn), so much swift change in the marketplace. How can people lift themselves above the noise?

And when you do attract new customers, they often bolt at the slightest hint of a better deal down the street. Word of mouth, which is so essential to business success, never gets off the ground. It's a constant game of catch-up, missed goals, back-to-the-drawing-board, and perpetual boom and bust. Despite adhering to marketing and sales "best practices," nothing seems to help.

Yet a magic bullet does exist: the "expert's edge."

Though all entrepreneurs and companies are experts, few of them exploit their expertise to superior advantage. Those few who do rise above the so-called level playing field to assume higher places are a breed apart known as "thoughtleaders." No longer mere "specialists," "practitioners," "professionals," or even "experts," thoughtleading experts cease wondering where their next business meal will come from. Instead, they steadily welcome new customers from an ever-expanding prospect base that seeks them out, rather than the other way around.

As I introduce it here, does this concept of thoughtleading ring a bell? If not, join the crowd. You may have heard the term used here or there to describe some celebrity business author or speaker. But you probably never considered it a business strategy that you too could adopt. Yet becoming a thoughtleader is indeed within your reach if only you understand how to make it happen. This book will lead you through the right steps for doing just that.

And what a worthwhile journey it will be! Not only can thoughtleading as a business strategy pay huge dividends, but, once you have adopted it, your competitors will gradually shrivel away. Each passing day, week, month, and year, the health of your business will grow ever stronger. You'll grab larger and larger shares of your market.

Referrals will increase; your income will increase; loyalty will solidify. And unless your competitors also embrace thoughtleading as a strategy (and most of them will not), no other approach will help them. The gap will keep widening as you literally separate yourself from the competitive pack.

Why, then, do so few companies and individual entrepreneurs take advantage of the thoughtleading approach? Why do so many resist, or ignore, this formidable strategy?

Simple ignorance is one explanation. Most entrepreneurs and business experts haven't the slightest clue as to how to get started. Nor do they understand thoughtleading's dramatic capacity to transform. Many fail to recognize that this amazing strategy even exists.

When ignorance isn't the issue, a no less intimidating barrier blocks the way. Call it self-doubt, lack of confidence, or taking one's expertise for granted: too many entrepreneurs and specialists simply discount their own uniqueness. They may have achieved magnificent results and even breakthroughs for their clients and customers over the years, yet they consider themselves nothing special. "Hey, with the right training, a shoe salesman could do what I do," they lament.

Their low self-image can express itself in the form of denigrating questions:

- What's so different about the way I do things?
- What could I say that hasn't been said before?
- Don't lots of people do what I do?
- What's so unique (or original) about my ideas?
- What do I know about writing a book (or an article)?
- Why would someone come and listen to me give a talk?
- Why would a reporter care about interviewing me?
- Do I even have what it takes?

Such questions can haunt even the most accomplished of experts, causing secret musings about writing a book or giving a keynote speech to get shoved aside immediately. It's just too painful to dwell upon them.

The self-deprecating expert thus keeps to the familiar and the routine. Business development never escapes the prison walls of the old standbys of networking, cold calling, direct-mail campaigns, and paid advertising. Experts who are trapped in this loop end up being less creative than in their earlier days, less energized, less committed—and less happy. Presuming that thoughtleading is not for them sets them in an opposite dynamic. Self-fulfilling negativity and low morale become the order of the day, every day. Work is just a job, making a living, nothing special. They long ago gave up having a mission to always strive for and operate at their best.

Acquainting Yourself with "ing"

You are reading this book because your goal is to stop being like that. You've promised yourself that you will break through such self-imposed limitations. But before we proceed further, let's define a few basic terms I'll be using as we examine what you can and should do to achieve such goals.

Let's begin with a new word for your success vocabulary: *thoughtleader*. While it's normally written as "thought leader," we're combining the two words in order to convey the focused, singular concept that it really is.

If you are a leading thinker in your field, for example, you are a thoughtleader.

If you are already considered a "go-to" authority in your area of expertise, you are a thoughtleader.

If you're a professional with a high level of knowledge in your field, you are a thoughtleader.

If you're a professional services practitioner (attorney, consultant, or CPA, for example) whom others seek out for advice, you are a thoughtleader.

If you're a manager or corporate leader who consistently gets things done, you are a thoughtleader.

Basically, when your colleagues, prospects, and customers view you as one very smart guy or gal to know, you are a thoughtleader!

To leverage this status successfully, however, you'll next need to acquaint yourself with the letters *ing*. Genuine thoughtleaders are kinetic, daring, freewheeling, and inventive. They do things, think things, and try things. They don't sit around all day soaking up the limelight. They thoughtlead.

Adding an "ing" activates the concept, transforming it into both a verb and an adjective. Throughout the pages of this book, you'll learn how genuine thoughtleaders live that "ing" every moment of every day. By turning the concept of thoughtleadership into a proactive process, they electrify their otherwise lost-in-a-crowd status with a powerful, no-holds-barred expert's edge.

What specific thoughtleading actions and tools does this proactivity produce? You'll learn about them in this book, manifested as five thoughtleading pillars. You'll learn how to develop and wield these actions to your advantage, and how to keep your tools in tip-top shape so that they're ready to use when you need them. We'll start with the "pillar of all pillars," writing and publishing, for this pillar will build your thoughtleading muscle. The other four pillars then splay out from there, fitting together with Pillar 1 like fingers in a smart, stylish glove. Specifically, you'll learn how and why to

- Speak publicly to groups
- Originate, via research, "fresh" thinking
- Vigorously use the media
- Creatively leverage the Internet

Thoughtleading exercises the thoughtleader virtually every waking moment. When problems cannot be solved easily, your thoughtleading frame of mind will refuse to let you let them go, forcing you to dig deeper, insisting that you figure out the problem. Frequently, this leads to a solution that you previously might never have even imagined.

While working with your clients, you'll also sometimes find yourself bravely opposing a client's wrong-headed assumptions despite your natural fears that this means that your client might fire you for speaking your mind. While presenting your ideas to an audience, you'll stop worrying about how audience members will evaluate you, freeing yourself up even to alienate them if that's what it takes to challenge them with important ideas.

Thoughtleading as action turns brainstorming, experimenting, eurekas, and even failure into fodder for your next book or research project. Genuine thoughtleaders hang on even to seemingly half-baked ideas, if only because—who knows?—a seed of something different and vital just might be in there. Your thoughtleading frame of mind will thus cheer you on as you matter-of-factly risk all odds for the potentially impactful insights your crazy risks might bring you. In addition, thoughtleading as action will dynamize your own expertise, elevating it to such heights that you the thoughtleader are soon transformed into the one and only go-to authority that precisely the right people for you (i.e., your target prospects) begin turning to every time—and referring their friends to!

For those who choose thoughtleading, old, inferior ways of business development and doing business will fall by the wayside as clients and customers climb aboard your train eagerly and remain there. They'll stay because they appreciate your excellent value, and they'll stay because you deliver that value consistently. They'll also stay because they'll want more of it, and they'll be willing to pay handsomely for it again and again and again. None of them will give the slightest thought to running out and down the street to a nearby competitor. That's because no serious alternative to you will be anywhere in sight.

Acknowledgments

CONTRARY TO POPULAR PERCEPTION, writing a book is rarely a solitary endeavor. Though the occasional novelist or poet might prove the exception, thinking everything up in your head, with no input whatsoever from the outside world, is essentially impossible.

For a nonfiction book, help takes a variety of forms, each of which is much appreciated. Thus I express my grand appreciations for this book to:

Donya Dickerson, my editor, who jumped behind this book's concept from the get-go, championing it before all comers and working with me faithfully to make it happen. Thanks for being there, Donya, from beginning to end.

Ethel Cook and Curtis Bingham, my consultant comrades who conducted and compiled many of the interviews in this book, without which so many insights would've been missed. Thanks for meeting the challenge of such a formidable task.

Alan Weiss, author of *Million Dollar Consulting* and over 20 other books, a shining thoughtleader general in a nonthoughtleader world. Your inspiring example and your Million Dollar Consulting College got me finally running in the right direction. Thanks for turning on your light, Alan.

Madeline Vellturo, my stellar admin/scribe, who researched material and quotes for the chapters, organized my unwieldy notes, and helped me as well with who knows what else. Thanks for keeping my mind intact and my office uncluttered.

My great 2007 college interns Michaela St. Onge and Charlotte Cutter for reviewing my manuscript, checking facts when I asked, and brainstorming whatever I needed. Thanks for so many "little" things that in fact can grow to be quite big.

Bob and Doris Litwak, the world's best in-laws, ever supportive and encouraging and enthused. Your positive energies only bring out the best.

Finally, my sweet inspirations Barb and Chloe, the great loves of my life. Thanks for everything.

the
expert's
edge

1

Thoughtleading Today
and in Days Past

*He who refuses to embrace a unique opportunity loses
the prize as surely as if he had failed.*

WILLIAM JAMES

THE BEST-KNOWN THOUGHTLEADERS of today are megastars. You see
them on the covers of their books; you see them on TV. They are
quoted and profiled and spotlighted incessantly—not just in the business pages of newspapers and magazines, but in gossip columns and
society pages and on celebrity TV newsmagazines as well. They are
beyond famous—they are gargantuan glitterati, celebrated personali-
ties, ubiquitous, razzle-dazzle, neon-escent.

Consider the most glaring example, Donald Trump. The Donald
holds press conferences, writes bestsellers, shows up on Larry King and
Access Hollywood and *The View.* He has had his own hit TV show; he's

hosted *Saturday Night Live*. The *New York Times*, the *Wall Street Journal*, the *New York Post*, and *USA Today* all love him. He keynotes the most spectacular business events while he feuds with glitterati, leading the headlines on *Entertainment Tonight* and *Access Hollywood* and the covers of *Us* magazine, *Entertainment Weekly*, and *People*. Obviously, we could go on and on.

There is so much media to go around these days that thoughtleaders, when they make the *really* big time, can grow very large—oversized even. Yet this bigness isn't what thoughtleading is all about; it just exposes how many thoughtleading channels exist today and how far things can sometimes get carried away. What's much more important for the sincere practitioner of thoughtleading to understand is that all these media and all these "visibility channels" exist to help get the word out about thoughtleaders and their businesses. Knowing which media to use and how to use them is the key to thoughtleading success, even if one's fame or notoriety comes nowhere close to that of The Donald and other megastars.

What in fact is The Donald's core message? Do all his TV appearances, public feuds, and participation in high-profile events shine a spotlight on it—or do they serve to obscure it? One might presume that his message is something like this: "Wealth is good; wealth makes you free; wealth makes life fun." Wife 1, Ivana, thus leads logically to wife 2, Marla Maples, and thence to wife 3, Melania. Oh, and The Donald himself, well, he's just plain the best. The medium (Trump) has firmly established itself as the message (Trump's life), to resurrect the words of one of history's premier thoughtleaders, Marshall McLuhan: one achieves a Trump-like life by behaving like, and by actually *being*, Donald Trump. That is, the fact of his over-the-top lifestyle is his message, as opposed to uniquely developed thoughts about business success and the like.

Of course, The Donald's many bestsellers do provide morsels to consume. With titles like *The Art of the Deal*, *How to Get Rich*, *The Art of the Comeback*, and *The Way to the Top*, how could they not? Throughout their hardcover pages, Trump's musings on management, leadership, talent, career motivation, and global business lead the way.

In a passage about the need to continually monitor the potential of people in your organization, he writes: "Very often, your resources are greater than you might think. I don't like it when people underestimate me, and I try not to underestimate anyone else, either. People are multifaceted, and it's important to let them function in a way that will allow them to shine. Most people would rather succeed than fail, but sometimes the leader has to be the catalyst for putting 'success' into their personal vocabulary."

In another passage, about negotiation, Trump explains:

> *The best negotiators are chameleons. Their attitude, demeanor, approach and posture in a negotiation will depend on the person on the other side of the table. If the other party to the transaction wants to acquire something you own, let them convince you that you really don't want it or need it. In doing so, they'll convince you of just how badly they want it.*
>
> *Money is not always the only consideration for exchange in the sales of an asset. Think beyond the traditional boundaries. Learn the value of saying no. View any conflict as an opportunity.*

So The Donald's books do convey some personalized thinking on relevant business matters, forged from his own unique experiences and perspective. But does the typical Donald Trump TV appearance or sound bite include similar thoughtleading gems? Rarely—if ever.

Most other business thoughtleaders fare better, consistently staying on message whenever they show up to speak or be interviewed or otherwise face a microphone or a camera. Perhaps this is because, mercifully, they are *not* pursued by the paparazzi. They are in the public eye, yes, but it's the narrower lens of the business public eye, where stars can be stars within reason. Consider these names: Tom Peters, Rosabeth Moss Kanter, Harvey MacKay, Stephen Covey, Malcolm Gladwell, Joline Godfrey, Jim Collins, Michael Hammer, James Champy, Charles Garfield, David Maister, Adrian Slywotsky. Most of the public, the business public included, probably couldn't pick these people out of a police lineup or be sure who they were even when they were standing behind a lectern. Quite a few of these names you might even feel the need to look up!

The superstardom of most such business thoughtleaders lends itself to a more measured, more contained, more precise use of thoughtleading channels to help them spread their words. In Trump's world, by contrast, the writing of a book is only one plank in a larger-scale razzle-dazzle platform extravaganza. The book feeds into guest spots on dozens of network TV venues, which in turn shamelessly plug *The Apprentice*, which in turn shamelessly hawks Trump products (spring water, DVDs, Melania's clothing line). The end result? A visibility for Donald Trump's business ventures that leads even otherwise cautious, careful megabank officers, who should know better, to get on board the next Trump Tower in New York, Chicago, Los Angeles, or wherever else he decides to break new ground.

A book by a lesser thoughtleader, however, means something else: it is the culmination of hard, important work, a lengthy, solitary process of quiet research and reflection, a compilation and reporting of considered conclusions. It will serve as a gateway to the next stage of such thoughtleading, where the implications of the new insights will be absorbed and digested by professionals who might benefit from them. It's light-years away from the quick flash and buzz of a 30-second *Access Hollywood* celebrity bite, where scant seconds later all is forgotten as Paris Hilton or Lindsay Lohan bursts back upon the screen. For the glitterless thoughtleader, the motivation of all this careful reflection is to leave behind something that matters.

Consider Tom Peters as a clear example. Around 1980, he and Robert H. Waterman, both recently departed from McKinsey Consulting, designed a book concept around interviews they had done at McKinsey with companies around the world for the purpose of determining what makes organizations successful and "excellent." What do the best-performing companies actually do to get that way? And how could other firms that are lower on the totem pole learn from them and follow suit?

When the dust of their research settled, Peters and Waterman had identified 43 firms that they felt had significant lessons to share, a list that included Disney, Xerox, IBM, and Data General. The resulting pivotal conclusion was that business problems could be solved very effectively with as little business process "overhead" as possible. One ingredient for success, for example, in which few less successful companies at that time engaged, was the willingness to authorize people at all levels on the organizational chart to make decisions that would solve customer problems right there on the spot, without the need to ask a boss or take the request to a committee or to senior management. Peters and Waterman referred to this as "getting on with it." Porters at the Ritz (one of the companies studied), for instance, could execute an otherwise management-level decision (up to a specified dollar amount) without asking permission from a supervisor or from the hotel manager. This might take the form of a complimentary breakfast or switching a guest to a different room.

After submitting their manuscript to a publisher, the two new ex-McKinsey-ites hoped to get their insights out to as much of the business community as possible. After all, if the companies profiled in the book could benefit so greatly from such practices, maybe Peters and Waterman's little report could help a few other firms as well. No one, of course, author and publisher alike, imagined what was about to happen.

The book became an instant bestseller. Millions of copies and many years later, it is still going strong. Today, it's high on the list of the biggest-selling business books of all time. Although many of the firms cited have since seen their fortunes twist backward and/or rise and fall many times over, *In Search of Excellence's* stories and insights have led millions of company managements to reexamine their business procedures and adopt simpler or more empowering practices, which they later swear spurred them on to higher echelons of sweet success.

And what did this do for Peters and Waterman? Waterman went on to publish subsequent books with such titles as *The Renewal Factor: How the Best Get and Keep the Competitive Edge* and *The Frontiers of Excellence: Learning from Companies That Put People First.* Peters has published many subsequent books too, most of them bestsellers, and thanks to a series of PBS specials based on *In Search of Excellence* has even achieved a Trump-like recognizability, at least within the greater business community, albeit one that is far less glitzy. Of all our serious thoughtleaders today, Peters may be the only one whose name and face approach some level of popular recognition.

THOUGHT NOTES

True thoughtleaders keep working their thoughtleading channels until they find the right one that does the trick. The key to the expert's edge can take many forms.

Tony Robbins, for example, despite early sales success with his first book, *Unlimited Power*, still found mega-fame eluding him. Only after he embarked on a TV promotional campaign based on infomercials, the vast majority of which were broadcast in the wee hours of the morning, did things finally begin taking off for Tony.

Martha Stewart, too, despite writing many articles for the *New York Times* and a column for *House Beautiful*, became the household name she is today only thanks to continued appearances on the *Today* show. Her books, videotapes, CDs, and many personal appearances all helped, of course, but not until millions of viewers had experienced her personally on NBC in the mornings did she "seal the deal."

However, these examples should not be interpreted to mean that TV is thoughtleading's magic bullet. Both Robbins and Stewart are vying for a wider consumer audience than the majority of business thoughtleaders, whose target markets are typically far narrower. Electronic media (TV and radio) tend to perform poorly when one is trying to reach tighter audiences. So although TV and radio can help out by augmenting more primary thoughtleading pillars (publishing and speaking in particular), resist the impulse to skip over the fundamentals. Without these (books especially), even Tony and Martha would've failed to make the big time.

Revitalizing Assumptions

While Tom Peters may have achieved greater name recognition and perhaps a more populous following than the majority of his thoughtleader peers, he joins all of them in engaging in the same basic process of true thoughtleading: discovery (research), insight (conclusions), synthesis (book or article writing), communication and discourse (public speaking), and missionary zeal (promotion via media and the Internet). You could create your own list of favorite thoughtleaders similar to Tom, those who are well enough known to face the challenge of balancing notoriety and serious engagement in the process as best they can, but my list would be topped by Rosabeth Moss Kanter, Harvey Mackay, and the legend himself, the late great Peter Drucker.

Harvard Business School Professor Rosabeth Moss Kanter, for example, is widely reputed to be the first woman in academia to achieve the status of "management thoughtleader." Much of her renown stems from her emphasis on such issues as change management and employee empowerment, two environmental dynamics that she has helped to move from the sidelines to center stage through her 30-plus years of advocacy. It would not be reaching to suggest that Kanter's focus on these issues single-handedly pushed them to the top of the business world's agenda.

Kanter has published 16 books so far, beginning with an initial in-depth study of 1960s communes, which led to her debut under the decidedly businessy title of *The Men and Women of the Corporation*. This early focus set the stage for her thoughtleading in the decades that have followed. Consider her recommendations for business in the pages of one of her more recent books, *e-Volve!*, published in 2001:

"The Internet could produce a great leap forward to a shared consciousness around the world and connect peoples everywhere. . . . The best businesses in the digital world will be those that foster community internally and serve communities externally." She then lists the following qualities as required for business success in a new millennium immersed in digital commerce:

- Curiosity and imagination
- Good communication skills, near and far
- A cosmopolitan mindset, not confined to a single worldview
- Grasping complexity and finding the connections
- Caring about feeding people's bodies and spirits

These kinds of sentiments were hallmarks of 1960s communalists, and they provided Kanter's ongoing research with a thematic thread. Yet this is not to say that her discoveries are stale or outdated. Every new book she produces carries a fresh batch of data that can be used to paint a picture of the current world and translate it into advice and admonitions for practicing strategists and managers. Her book titles over the years reflect hard issues that need to be tackled head on if a company is to maintain its competitive edge. Observe:

- *Work and Family in the United States*, about diversity and work-family balance
- *When Giants Learn to Dance*, about mastering the new terms of engagement for competing in a global information-based marketplace
- *Confidence: How Winning Streaks and Losing Streaks Begin and End*, which compares the culture and dynamics of high-performance organizations with those of organizations in decline
- *World Class: Thriving Locally in the Global Economy*, identifying the rise of new business networks and the benefits and tensions of globalization

It's precisely this kind of basic research that enables managers and other business leaders to make sense of their ever-churning corporate environments. In this way, they revitalize their assumptions and keep their organizations driving forward, despite the rise of hurdles never encountered before. The thoughtleading of Rosabeth Moss Kanter sharpens their senses.

Rooted in Experience

Also leading the charge for change over the past few decades is Harvey Mackay, an envelope manufacturer who first burst upon the scene decades ago with the provocatively titled book *Swim with the Sharks without Being Eaten Alive*. This first book made its way to the top of the *New York Times* bestseller list like a rocket and hung there for months and months, well over a year. Since then, Mackay has banged out unique business and career concepts in a dozen subsequent books whose total sales have now surpassed 10 million. Translated into 37 languages, his ideas have reached readers in 80 countries.

Although Harvey Mackay's academic credentials include a B.A. from the University of Minnesota and graduation from the Executive Program at Stanford University's Graduate School of Business, his focus on how to achieve excellent customer service, effectiveness in business management, and ideas for advancing one's career stem from a different discovery/research source than do those of Rosabeth Moss Kanter. Rather than conducting surveys and studies to formulate his thoughtleading recommendations, MacKay instead tends to draw more from direct experience.

At age 26, for example, he purchased a small, unsuccessful envelope company in Minnesota that today, over 45 years later, as a result of his innovative efforts, grosses $85 million annually. His first book, *Swim with the Sharks*, detailed the trials and tribulations endured during this transformation, primarily focusing on Mackay's homegrown take on implementing superior customer service.

"Our company motto," he has repeatedly said, "is 'Do what you love . . . love what you do . . . and deliver more than you promise.'" As one proof that this works, Mackay submits (with a justified measure of pride) that over close to five decades, his Mackay Envelope Corporation has never, ever lost a major account. The company's manic dedication to its customers, he explains, is the reason why.

"Anyone, any salesperson, can get one order, but the mark of true salesmanship is not to get one order but to get and keep an account," he says on his Web site, www.harveymackay.com. "You can exaggerate or actually make misrepresentations and you can get an order that takes no talent whatsoever. But it takes enormous talent to be able to *keep* a customer."

Such insight is rooted in Mackay's personal experiences, as life's hard knocks form the basis for his expansive body of thoughtleading. As a result, today Mackay routinely delivers keynote speeches and wisdom to leaders of Fortune 500 companies, Ivy League university chancellors, and the highest level of major government institutions. His books since *Swim with the Sharks* have also been bestsellers, his name is possibly just as well known in "business households" as Tom Peters's, and the clamor for his perspective seems in no danger of ever letting up.

Still the Youngest Mind

If there were a Thoughtleader Mt. Olympus, the late Peter Drucker would probably have all the other thoughtleaders, including stars like Peters, Kanter, and Mackay, sitting at his feet. Serious students of management agree that Drucker was the quintessential thoughtleader and in fact could be fairly acknowledged as the thoughtleader who started it all.

Drucker passed away in November 2005 at the age of 95, but he had adorned the cover of *Forbes* magazine less than 10 years earlier (when he was 87) under a banner that proclaimed: "Still the Youngest Mind." *BusinessWeek* labeled him "the most enduring management thinker of our time." Countless other publications, authors, corporate leaders, and consulting gurus have celebrated him in the same way.

Most of Drucker's 40 books focus on business subjects, although his most devoted followers would point out that his first book focused not on business at all, but on politics and society. Yet it was his conclusions about political dynamics that earned him an invitation to observe the inner workings of General Motors, at that time (1945) one of the largest companies in the world, and ultimately resulted in Drucker's notoriety. The business book that followed, *The Concept of the Corporation*, made GM's multidivisional organizational structure famous, putting both GM and Drucker on the map.

After that, Drucker's thoughtleading influence just grew and grew. His numerous articles, columns, national and international consulting engagements, and additional books spread his gospel of effective leadership practices as well as his continued fascination with how such practices must evolve in the face of unexpected change. He saw himself not as a mere reporter of change or an impartial researcher-advisor, but instead as an in-your-face hurler of challenges. He insisted that business leaders not only hear what he had to say but go out and do something about it.

In the 1950s, for example, the rise of the "knowledge professional" caught his attention and never let go. Many workers of that time, Drucker observed, knew as much as (or more than) their superiors. So he began decrying traditional hierarchies as outdated, advocating instead a transformation of corporate structures from Industrial Age formats to something more conducive to productivity based on intellect.

In today's world, then, Peter Drucker lives on despite his passing not only because of his vast and respected thoughtleading research, but also because his thoughtleading energies did not stop there. It was not enough for Drucker to point something out; he wanted his followers to apply new knowledge to their own business environments and then go the next step by taking action. His expertise was meaningless within a context of inaction and an unwillingness to risk failure by trying something new. For this reason, Drucker remains the light for modern-day thoughtleaders to follow.

Emerson and Other Thoughtleaders in Concord

In days gone by, of course, there have been other lights to follow, no less insistent and no less bright. One could thumb through history and uncover many such pioneers whose flames have lit candles and even bonfires, causing their thoughtleading ideas to burst forth with fire and heat and blinding light. Consider Aristotle, Socrates, and Plato; consider Voltaire, Galileo, and John Locke; consider Ben Franklin, Thomas Jefferson, and Sam Adams; consider Joan of Arc; consider Confucius; consider Marie Curie, Albert Einstein, Thomas Edison, and Alexander Graham Bell.

Thousands of gigantic volumes would be needed to adequately recount the activities of all these thoughtleaders, or even to just list all their names. But their own fears and mad thoughts and insane experiments have given us a legacy. Most of them were not even business types, yet their thoughtleading has paved the way for our own contrarian states of mind.

Consider Emerson. Though not a businessman per se, Ralph Waldo Emerson's life practices have laid the foundation for today's business thoughtleading way of life. Any business thoughtleader today, any expert seeking the expert's edge, would do well to adopt a typical Emerson weekly schedule.

World-renowned in the mid-nineteenth century for his essays and books, Emerson's stature as a leading thoughtleader of his day was quite secure. In addition to buying and reading such books and essays as *Nature*, *Self-Reliance*, and *The Law of Compensation*, many of his fans thought nothing of embarking on a journey of many hours or days to make their way to Concord, Massachusetts, and drop in to see him. The present-day Concord Museum offers a rich account of a band of Harvard students who trekked out from Cambridge, Massachusetts, some 20 miles away, in a blinding snowstorm to pay an uninvited visit to the "Sage of Concord" and bask in his presence, asking him about subjects that were not covered fully in his books. And Emerson gracefully welcomed them to his hearth and spent the evening with them in study and discussion.

In much the same way, Emerson often traveled to the homes of his thoughtleader contemporaries, although it's likely that he let them know he was coming! In that same Cambridge lived Henry Wadsworth Longfellow, whom Emerson communicated with (by letters) frequently and knew well. A thoughtleader in his own right, Longfellow also networked with thoughtleader comrades of the day, joining Emerson, for example, at the Parker Hotel in Boston on many Saturdays for what they all called the "Saturday Club," a no-holds-barred all-day philosophy fest frequented by a conclave of Victorian Age Boston deep thinkers. Regulars included Bronson Alcott (Louisa May's dad), Nathanial Hawthorne, Oliver Wendell Holmes, and the esteemed poet James Russell Lowell.

But the sessions offered more than philosophical debates. There was also time for brainstorming literary ideas, passing on the names of good (and bad) book publishers, sharing advice on finances and commerce, and supporting one another in their quest to resolve obstacles, fears, and dilemmas. Presumably, this helped all of them get and stay successful in their various endeavors, and it shows how little professional life has changed in 160 years. Today we are told to network, network, network and to join professional groups and seek out feedback and support. Critical advice then and now.

By the same token, top thoughtleaders generations ago sought out the expert's edge via peer interaction and networking, as well as other thoughtleading actions. Emerson's writing, for example, though it was the foundation of his fame, was *not* the sole focus of his day-to-day work, primarily because writing alone, as is still frequently true today, could not financially support him. So for four to six months out of each year he hit the road, by stagecoach or the newfangled train, to tour America's cities, towns, and villages and speak at their lyceums and meeting halls. Adding this public speaking pillar of thoughtleading to his writing and networking, he presented his ideas in person, educating his audiences and fans, debating with them, provoking them, even unsettling them. In this way, Emerson made enough income to support himself and his family, and to allow him to spend the remaining months of each year developing his thoughtleading ideas.

What else did it do? Each lyceum visit, each carefully constructed and precisely delivered lecture, each rousing debate with a cantankerous farmer or feisty village highbrow helped him refine his own ideas as well as expand the world's knowledge of him. His talks made his books sell, got his essays read, and spurred word of mouth the next day at the water cooler (or more accurately, in Emerson's day, the horse troughs).

If Emerson's hope was that his beloved writing would expand thinking and knowledge and the general consciousness, his speaking pushed that goal 10 paces ahead and kept it moving. For the same reasons, to achieve a similar expert's edge, today's thoughtleaders must activate the same one-two punch of publishing and speaking for both personal and business advantage. The process of thoughtleading is organic: as we see with the thoughtleaders of today like Peters, Kanter, Mackay, and Drucker—and, yes, even The Donald—Emerson's propensity to think, write, speak, and network served him and those who learned from him on many fronts. Done in this way, thoughtleading serves all who incorporate it into their natural operational lives so that ideas can be germinated, grown, and harvested for the benefit of both those who reap and those who sow.

What about Thoreau?

Those of you who know your transcendentalists may be wondering why I'm making such a big deal about Ralph Waldo Emerson and ignoring his even better-known contemporary Henry David Thoreau. Well, that's a fair question that's worth exploring.

Although Emerson is quoted ubiquitously these 150-plus years later, the same can be said of Thoreau. Certainly a case could be made that Thoreau's impact as a thoughtleader has been, over this period of time, even more pronounced and far-reaching than Emerson's. After all, his writings on civil disobedience influenced both Gandhi and

Martin Luther King and literally millions of others throughout the latter nineteenth century, the twentieth, and now the twenty-first.

Thoreau's epic two years, two months, and two days in a small cabin that he built with his own hands (on land donated by Emerson, by the way) on the shore of Walden Pond is still hailed as possibly the prime inspiration for such popular uprisings as the environmental movement, the back-to-the-land movement, the hippie movement, the human potential movement, conservation, antimaterialism, and vegetarianism. Moreover, Thoreau did write about and speak out on such social-political issues of the day as slavery (quite against it), the Mexican War (also against), the increasingly hectic pace of day-to-day life (against), and technology (those loud, polluting steam engines gave him the willies).

Unquestionably Thoreau was a thoughtleader, and one whose impact is still being felt in resounding tones all over our globe. But where Thoreau differs from Emerson is in his dedication to personal independence, i.e., to going his own way. Not insignificantly, he was not particularly a lover of society either.

Though he did mix with Emerson's family, with the Alcotts, and with his own (actually very close) family, in the end all the supper parties, odd jobs, lecturing, and attendance at speeches at the Concord Lyceum took a backseat to his own self. He loved to amble around Walden Woods, canoe down the Concord and Merrimac Rivers, trek off to Mt. Katahdin in Maine, tramp over the windswept sand dunes of Cape Cod, or make an "excursion" to Quebec, the Great Lakes, Philadelphia, or even New York City. Sometimes his brother went with him. Most times, though, he went his way alone.

It would thus be fair to say that Thoreau was not nearly the dedicated networker that Emerson was, nor did he care much for either career or business. Other than a few years when he worked at his family's pencil factory, he rarely showed much ambition for conventional work. So yes, although he surely was a grand thoughtleader, and quite an impactful one at that, Emerson is the better model for our purposes. It was Emerson who could find value in integrating his thoughtleading actions with professional goals for himself—just as most of us are attempting to do today.

While adopting a thoughtleader strategy can manifest itself in a variety of ways, from the flamboyance of Donald Trump to the solitariness of Thoreau, it's that middle ground displayed by Tom Peters, Rosabeth Moss Kanter, Harvey Mackay, and Ralph Waldo Emerson that counts for us the most. The "fame" created by your expert's edge must not create a gulf between you and your target market. Its purpose instead is to make you *more* accessible so that those who are looking for your kind of service see you and you alone as the go-to authority to turn to first, last, and always. In Chapter 2, we'll examine why this translates, happily, into an ability to dramatically increase your income.

2

The ROI of Thoughtleading

Why Experts with an Edge
Make the Most Money

Boldness in business is the first, second, and third thing.

HENRY GEORGE BOHN

So THOUGHTLEADING AS A STRATEGY sounds good and feels good and
looks good. It sounds logical that it would work productively to deliver
a competitive advantage, but how can we know for sure? Examples of
thoughtleaders such as Donald Trump, Tom Peters, Rosabeth Moss
Kanter, and Harvey Mackay—and even Ralph Waldo Emerson—
demonstrate that it can work for some people, but can it work for you
and me as well?

The more quantitatively oriented among us will put it more
bluntly: Can you prove it? Is there evidence that thoughtleading in fact
really does produce measurable business growth? Can metrics be cited?
Is there a way to identify thoughtleading's return on investment (ROI)?

Although the answers to these questions are all yes, the path to getting there, like so much else in life, requires a map. Studies of thoughtleading do indeed indicate that there is a quantifiable return on investment as a result of this strategy. Some of these studies are direct and dramatic. Others, however, may feel murkier to our quantitatively minded friends. Yet the research exists, and its results are overwhelmingly affirmative.

To get to the heart of the truest answer to the question of thoughtleading's ROI, we must first understand that old ways of measuring ROI may not apply here. That's because there's a new equation in our economy, one that's harder to see, mistier, and more vague than the traditional bottom-line measurement (dollars spent divided by dollars returned), one that requires new ways of measurement. We're talking about the economic asset of *intellectual capital (IC)*. While the concrete but now-aging ROI metric based on I-can-see-it-with-my-own-eyes still applies to material goods, IC's decidedly non-Industrial Age elements can be harder to fathom. Mary Adams, managing principal of Trek Consulting LLC, explains why:

> *Can you imagine a merchant without an inventory report, having to sell product without knowing the quantity or price of goods he owns? Yet this is the position that most corporate leaders are in today. They lack basic consolidated information about their most important resources: Do we have the right people, network, and knowledge to meet our goals? Are we positioned for continued innovation? Where are we at risk?*

An expert in the rapidly growing new field of intellectual capital, Adams maintains that boards of directors, investors, and analysts are all adrift in the same leaky boat. "They are forced to analyze the future potential of a company with incomplete and inconsistent information," she says, an information gap that produces such nothing statements by corporate leaders as:

- We have great people.
- We have the best technology available.

- Our IP is a core advantage.
- We have close relationships with our customers.

Yet company leaders get away with such vacuosities because those listening to them are clueless about ways to provide objective information on intangible resources. Today, even for an "industrial" company like GE, intellectual capital is more important than in years past, driving everything from innovation to earnings to growth to competitive advantage. Though information about intellectual capital can be found scattershot in most companies, with HR groups tracking personnel, and with marketing and sales gathering CRM data on the firm's customers, Adams notes that none of these items typically appear in one consolidated report.

"We are moving to a global, knowledge-based economy in which success is no longer about access to raw materials, machinery, and factories," she explains. "Today it's about a new kind of raw material that helps businesses build knowledge and innovation. And the traditional balance sheet is not equipped to provide this view of a company's potential because the most critical resources in the knowledge economy don't qualify for accounting treatment." Adams lists these critical intangible resources as

- Human capital, i.e., employees and managers
- Structural capital, i.e., knowledge, intellectual property, know-how, processes, systems, and software
- Relationship capital, i.e., brands and relationships with customers and external partners such as suppliers, distributors, and development partners

Leadership ROI

Along the same lines, attempts to measure ROI in similarly "soft" disciplines suggest that new perspectives are called for. One such attempt to measure the ROI of leadership has been developed by leader mentor Michael Shenkman, Ph.D., founder and president of the nationally recognized leader mentor consulting firm Arch of Leadership, based in Albuquerque and Boston. The author of such books as *Leader Mentoring* (Career Press), *The Arch and The Path: The Life of Leading Greatly* (Sandia Heights Media), *The Strategic Heart: Using the New Science to Lead Growing Organizations* (Greenwood Press), and *Value and Strategy: Competing Successfully in the Nineties* (Greenwood Press), Shenkman says that to make the case for leadership ROI, one must get away from the historical model employed for assessing return on investments for capital equipment and instead conceive new ways to measure your investment returns from the "immediate, day-to-day, across-the-board impacts" of leadership. In *Business Strategies 2007*, Shenkman and coauthor Bonnie Gorbaty state:

> *Every company today competes increasingly on its value proposition and the ways it is able to differentiate from the competition and away from commoditization. Value gets created in the development of products and services, in the right hiring and development of talent, in strategic market positioning to name a few of the big ones.*
>
> *But the real value that feeds into all of these is what leaders bring to the enterprise with their compelling visions, and their ability to integrate disparate ideas/solutions/opportunities into competitive advantages, and their energy in driving cross-functional innovation.*

How can such intangibles be measured?

Shenkman and Gorbaty refer to the book *Good to Great*, in which Jim Collins profiled 11 companies that achieved the leap suggested by his title. These firms averaged cumulative stock returns greater than 6.9 times the general market during a 15-year transition period. An investment in these 11 good-to-great companies during those 15 years would have multiplied 471 times, compared to a 56-fold increase in the broader market.

How did these 11 achieve this leap? They realized the value of leading, the authors insist, requiring a different kind of investing. Instead of investing in tools for efficiency, these 11 good-to-great firms invested over the longer term in appreciating and nurturing the talents and energies of their emerging leaders. As a result of this investment, they developed a "deep bench" of people across many disciplines who could be counted on to envision new approaches to the company's opportunities. They could also be counted on to enlist the energies of others effectively and robustly, so as to accomplish those approaches. No executive searches, no down time in training new people, no resentments from being passed over for promotions, no defections. "Just put the leaders you have developed in place, and run with it," Shenkman explains. "That's an ROI worth the price."

To Shenkman and Gorbaty, "appreciating and nurturing the talents and energies of emerging leaders" constitute a return-on-investment that's identifiable, impactful, and durable. Skeptics of course might reply that such arguments, though strong, nonetheless beg the question of a hard-and-fast formula for quantifying leadership ROI. In response, Shenkman and Gorbaty have in fact augmented their thesis with a quantifiable formula that factors into the equation such variables as executive salaries, stock prices, costs of executive searches, and marginal growth rates. Offering such a formula further weakens the argument that soft disciplines cannot be measured in hard dollars.

If leadership can be quantified, can other ROI for other soft disciplines such as thoughtleading and media attention and publishing be measured as well? Surprisingly, perhaps, the answer is yes.

Definite Measurements

Definite measurements of thoughtleading ROI that would satisfy even the most old-school quantifiability standards do exist. A 2003 study of law firms, for example, by Levick Strategic Communications of Chicago, in conjunction with *PR Newswire*, attempted to measure ROI in relation to the use of legal media. Counting up the media appearances of 200 law firms, Levick's survey found that the top 25 firms on its list ranked according to revenue also reported an 18 percent increase in overall media presence in the previous two years. Of firms ranked below this top tier, however, media presence had increased by only a minuscule 1 percent. Richard Levick, president of Levick Strategic Communications, interpreted these data as significant justification for investing in sustained media efforts.

Likewise, Kennedy Information, the nation's premiere management consulting think tank, headquartered in New Hampshire, has conducted surveys of revenue levels of practicing management consultants showing that less than 1 percent of such consultants typically attain compensation levels of $500,000 per year or more. At a PowerPoint presentation of these findings near Boston, two Kennedy presenters were asked, "What makes these consulting firms and individuals at the top so much better paid than all the rest?"

Without skipping a beat, one presenter replied, "Oh, those highest revenue producers are the ones who regularly publish articles and books. They are the thoughtleaders."

Integration Is Key

In addition to studies that correlate revenue with publishing, speaking, media, and other individual thoughtleading actions, a study by The Bloom Group, a professional services marketing firm, has found that thoughtleading's ROI will be measurably high when it is integrated with a firm's more traditional marketing and sales activities and other functions. Publishing articles, for example, can be incorporated into the marketing and selling pipeline, and sales reps can use published articles as tools for building credibility.

In a 2006 survey of 179 U.S. professional services firms that utilized thoughtleading actions, The Bloom Group study also found that, in all categories of marketing activities (articles, books, presentations, Webinars, etc.), marketing managers rated the effectiveness of these activities higher than did nonmarketing managers. However, the nonmarketing managers said six marketing activities were effective to vary-ing degrees: articles in company print publications, conference pre-sentations at third-party events, firm seminars, firm-bylined articles, Webinars, and e-mail newsletters. They also reported certain other activities that seemed to be ineffective to varying degrees for marketing thought leadership, such as advertising, sales brochures, Web site arti-cles, telemarketing, conference booths, and traditional PR. "I am skep-tical of the value of thoughtleading, period," was the general consensus of the firms' upper echelon, its senior executives, and managing prin-cipals. "All that stuff only takes time away from my billable hours" was the general consensus of practitioners overall.

Yet the ROI for such activities as advertising, which almost all of the firms engaged in (and at a very expensive rate), as well as for four-color brochures, dazzling Web sites, and glitzy embossed business cards, could not be measured at all! The notion that "everybody else is doing it" seemed enough to drive many marketing decisions (and expenditures) in all these highly traditional directions. As Bob Buday, a founding partner of The Bloom Group, observed, "Oddly, those actions that could be quantified as producing a discernible ROI were the thoughtleader activities: publishing books and articles, doing speaking engagements." Perhaps one relevant insight could be that since thoughtleading is typically *not* practiced by one's competitors, no similar keeping-up-with-the-Joneses therefore takes hold. Because oth-ers are not doing them, thoughtleading actions are not accorded much credibility.

Buday further explains that a thoughtleading ROI is especially measurable when various thoughtleading actions are integrated with traditional sales and marketing actions. Article ROI, for example, can be measured by having sales reps ask their prospects if the firm's pub-lished articles had played any part in either their initial decision to approach the company or their ultimate decision to do business with the company. Using an article within the sales process itself, in fact, can be an extremely effective tool as well, as demonstrated by Dan Cas-sidy, president of Cassidy Retirement Group Inc., in Concord, Massa-chusetts, a columnist for *Employee Benefits Plan Review* and author of the book *A Manager's Guide to Strategic Retirement Plan Management* (Wiley). As he explains

> *I always e-mail prospects a PDF or two of my published arti-cles early in the sales process, and I take along copies of my articles to face-to-face prospect meetings. I want to be able to hand a relevant article to a prospect at an appropriate point in the meeting so that the prospect will glance at it and be impressed. "Wow, this looks pretty cool," may be all the prospect says or does, then we move on. But that's sufficient to stamp my firm as something more than some run-of-the-mill small-guy consultancy, as a smaller firm that delivers the same if not better quality than a giant competitor, which is the way it is.*

Touch points in the marketing/sales process are very few, Cassidy feels, so to expand and maximize them, he integrates his book and arti-cles. "The typical consultant at a big firm doesn't write and publish articles and books as I do," he adds. "They just send big bills! That's a message that becoming a published thoughtleader allows me to send loud and clear."

High Use, High Success

A final source of evidence that thoughtleading ROI can be measured can be found in the work of Suzanne Lowe, president of Expertise Marketing. In her research measuring which marketing tactics work best, covered in her book *Marketplace Masters: How Professional Ser-vice Firms Compete to Win* (Greenwood Press), Lowe has identified thoughtleading actions as a major differentiator.

Sympathizing with the challenge of measuring intellect-based, intangible services, she cites ROI measurement as a traditional brick wall for professional services firms. She believes, however, that in the past 10 years, much has improved. Back a decade ago, in 1997, for example, only 23 percent of respondents to her annual surveys reported bothering to calculate a monetary ROI from their promotional vehicles. Also, "most of them were measuring only the initial and most easily trackable cash outlays, not other important ROI features such as investments in time and innovation."

Measuring clients' opinions and impressions of the firm and/or its marketing programs didn't get much more attention. Only 27 percent of Lowe's respondents 10 years ago reported using formal surveys and evaluation forms. More often, she says, they relied on anecdotal feedback and comments—not exactly rock-solid, compelling evidence!

Now, however, based on her 2006 research on measuring the effectiveness of marketing in professional firms, Suzanne reports that firms are poised to treat marketing ROI more seriously and "with more sophistication and commitment." To do it right, they need to rely less on measuring only their promotional activities and more on calculating their overall branding effectiveness. They also need to quit relying primarily on their gut in favor of focused attention on statistics displaying where their leads have come from, including which marketing actions produce qualified leads and which produce few such leads or none at all.

In her ongoing research, Lowe has found that some differentiation tactics that are in high use typically fall way down into the wrong quadrants of her marketing mastery grid. Others are firmly entrenched in quadrants labeled "High Use, High Success" or "Low Use, High Success." According to responses from surveys of professional services firms, many companies simply assume, for example, that developing a new positioning or adding techniques and tools to "deliver" their services better *must* be effective tactics, only to report, upon reflection, that these did not seem to help their cause much at all (low success).

Other techniques, such as the thoughtleading action of embarking on a public relations campaign, tend not to be as widely used, yet when they are used, they can prove far more effective than many "high-use" practices. Lowe found, for example, that only 30 percent of the companies she surveyed had embarked on a PR campaign, yet for those who did, this action found itself in a "high-success" quadrant.

"It turns out that firms tend to underestimate the impact of many marketing tactics," Lowe concludes. "When they measure them, however, the guesswork is gone and the facts speak for themselves."

THOUGHT NOTES

Too Narrow a Focus

"Too many firms measure only the tail end of their marketing efforts," Suzanne Lowe, author of *Marketplace Masters*, observes. This means they're focusing on promotional data, such as e-newsletter open rates. This is a double-edged sword because (on the positive side) one has to start the measurement engine somewhere, so why not at the tactical level? Indeed, it's good to see some of the bigger firms routinely measuring the ROI of their media coverage or new leads from client seminars, for example.

But for most of them, measurement for more significant strategic activities, such as whether their differentiation strategies are competitively effective, is simply not on the radar screen. Thus, Suzanne believes that measurements of thoughtleading and other marketing actions are typically conducted with too narrow a focus.

Impact from Anecdotes

Of course, anecdotal evidence too, while often not considered scientific enough to suit the most quantitatively oriented minds, will nonetheless impress many of the rest of us. In business, for example, there is rarely anything more convincing for a prospect than a concrete example or two of how a product or service really works. Customer testimonials can tip the scales too. Though only quantification will cinch the deal for the strictly numbers-minded left-brainers among us, firsthand stories of someone's success create vivid pictures of how it can also happen to us. Of course, hard metrics and colorful stories together will prove most convincing of all.

What anecdotes can thoughtleaders contribute to demonstrate the impact of thoughtleading actions on their bottom line? Here are a few to savor.

Establishing Credibility

Vin D'Amico, founder and president of Damicon LLC, author of numerous published articles, and columnist for the *Indus Business Journal*, reports:

> *In one contract I landed, I spoke with the prospect on the phone, then e-mailed a copy of my published article on disaster recovery. He read the article and told me, "Your article outlined exactly the things we need to do." Because of the article, he gave me an appointment and the resulting meeting led to the engagement. Having that article available helped the sales process enormously by establishing my credibility and eliminating the need for reference checks.*

THOUGHT NOTES

Identify "Indicators"

"Measuring your thoughtleading ROI involves asking this question: What would make this worth it to you?" says Mary Adams of Trek. What's the value of being considered an expert, being known as an expert, having your marketing materials certified and validated by an objective outsider?

Measurement should involve identifying "indicators" that you can track, indicators that will let you know that you are heading in the right direction. What's the level of quality of the publications that are publishing you? How many of your articles are getting accepted for publication? How many of your prospects are coming to you because of your articles, or because of your speaking engagements, or because of your e-letter? How many are commenting positively on your thoughtleading actions so that your credibility is rising? These indicators are measures of your thoughtleading ROI as well.

Clear Increase in Business Flow

One marketing manager for a client of mine, a midsized CPA firm whose managing partners regularly publish articles and vie for media attention, says the following:

> Before our firm started to regularly publish articles and get our accountants interviewed by business media, we handled only about 10 estate planning accounts per month. Even our clients didn't think of us when they needed someone to handle these matters for them. So we focused initially on raising the visibility of our ability to provide estate planning by writing articles about related topics and positioning ourselves to the media as estate planning experts. As a result, that section of our business is very robust now, with 50 to 60 cases in any given month, a growth rate of 400 to 500 percent.

Visible? Or IN-visible?

"Our thoughtleading program has made us more visible in the Boston media, whereas before we would see articles by or quoting our competitors' names there," says Sarah Crocker, director of client services for Wolf Greenfield, a leading IP law firm in Boston. "This visibility is important because it provides us with a venue for demonstrating our expertise to those who are not familiar with our firm."

Repositioning for a Major League Assignment

Jim Masciarelli, founder and CEO of PowerSkills Solutions and author of the book *PowerSkills: Building Top-Level Relationships for Bottom-Line Results* (Nimbus Press) reports:

> *A partner of a top venture capital firm who knew me from my past career as a retained executive search consultant called me up after receiving an announcement of my book* Power-Skills, *which details a system I created for building profitable business relationships.* "I understand you're now doing advisory and alignment work with CEOs and executive teams," *he said.* "We could use your help."
>
> *Their portfolio company had just bought a major Internet company in a $22 billion stock deal, but the CEO did not yet have a plan to integrate these companies. The mere announcement of my book and, with it, my new practice repositioned me in his mind to this new line of work I was now doing. As a result, I got the introduction to the CEO and ultimately the assignment as well.*

Solidifying Prospect Interest

Dave Vogel, founder and president of Intertech Engineering Associates, author of numerous published articles and a professional speaker and trainer, says the following:

> I always load my briefcase with all my published articles before going out on a sales call. I like to have one of everything ready. At the right time in a meeting, I pull out the right article, one that covers the particular service that this prospect has expressed most interest in. Doing so always helps to solidify the prospect's interest.
>
> On one sales call, I took along someone on my staff, an engineer whom I had previously invited to coauthor an article with me but who had shown little interest in doing so. He just couldn't see any great value in doing so, he told me. By the time we had left this sales meeting, however, his mind had changed.
>
> "If only we had that article to show him," he said. "A reprint would've sold them for sure."

To Win New Business, Post Articles on the Internet

Curtis Bingham, president of Predictive Consulting Group, author of numerous published articles, and frequent speaker and panelist at industry events, says:

> I obtained one corporate client that commissioned me to do a report on the value of the Chief Customer Officer (CCO), which is an area of expertise of mine. This firm had found me on the Web via an article I had published. It contacted me, and we arranged the assignment.

In another case, a large consulting firm also saw an article of mine on the Web, and called to ask if I was interested in developing a study focusing on Chief Customer Officers. This firm had been tasked by one of its clients with creating an Office of the Customer, an area it knew nothing about. But since I had already done such a study, the firm was able to save itself much time and trouble by merely purchasing a copy of my study, which in turn expanded my reputation as a thoughtleader in this new but growing trend in addition to earning me some extra income."

Thought Notes

Perceived Brilliance

"It's all about being smart when it comes to using what you know," explains Jim Durham, chief marketing officer at Ropes & Gray LLP. "People ask me if they should write a book; will it bring them business? Well, the book I cowrote and coedited for the ABA, *The Lawyer's Guide to Marketing Your Practice*, only brought me one direct engagement (that I know of) when I was consulting, but over three years that particular client paid me about $150K. And every time I competed for business, I was able to say, 'I wrote the book on marketing' for the ABA; and I could bring it out and show it off.

There's a 'perceived brilliance' there that prospects often respond to. Is there value in that? Sure! I also believe that the credibility that came with writing the book was helpful when I was interviewing with my current employer."

Tracking Is Key

Karen Wolf, marketing manager for Accenture, a management, technology, and outsourcing consulting firm that supports a thoughtleading program encompassing original research, publishing, and public speaking, explains:

> *The primary marketing objectives of our program are to drive awareness of our firm's human capital capabilities and establish more high-quality touch points with our clients and prospects. Our business goal is to grow Accenture's human capital business and gain mindshare in the human capital market by generating qualified leads.*
>
> *Our publishing activities are thoroughly survey-based and research-based. We begin the process by developing research hypotheses, then executing a telephone survey of C-level executives, then analyzing the resulting data, and finally developing our research-based point of view. After all that, we develop and publish a primary report and spinoff articles.*
>
> *How do we know that this approach delivers any concrete bottom-line results? For one thing, we methodically track the numbers of "hits" and "mentions" in the human capital Internet space, comparing ourselves to our competitors. Next, we correlate that with our business results, which have driven us upward to number one in all but one quarter of the last four years. Though IBM is on our tail, we're still out in front of them and everyone else.*
>
> *We've discovered from this a direct correlation between the number of channels out there that you use to reach a prospect and your prospects' awareness of you. If they're seeing and hearing about you in print publications, and seeing you at a seminar too, and getting materials in the mail, and you're showing up on the Internet—all of these have a direct impact on referrals and awareness, we've found.*

To achieve all these mentions and hits, the primary thing we take to the media is our thoughtleadership, which we keep generating continuously. We're constantly looking at what pieces of new thoughtleadership we have in process, and what ideas are in the pipeline for the next quarter. We're always working the pipeline. It keeps us ahead of the pack.

What Are You Aiming For?

If you want to combine quantifiability with anecdotal mental pictures, I point you next in the direction of my own experiences. Though I could cite a number of situations in which a certain tactic produced an ROI that was clearly high, and a like number of situations in which the ROI was low, it should be added that one simple question, often forgotten yet more revealing than any other, can help you zero in on the effectiveness of your thoughtleading actions. That question is: "How did you hear of us?" If enough clients answer that a thoughtleading action sent them your way, or if even one or two major-major clients came your way because of one thoughtleading action or another, your ROI in dollars from that action could be handsome enough to make all other measurements nice but, practically speaking, superfluous.

I can cite, for example, articles I have published that directly resulted in a significant paid keynote speaking engagement, and speaking engagements that have themselves resulted in additional well-paid or even better-paid speaking engagements. Or perhaps a speaking gig led to an invitation to write an article or to be interviewed for one, which in turn led to a major new client or another paid keynote engagement.

Sometimes the path from thoughtleading action to compensation is very direct, making it a breeze to quantify. Other times the path takes a few twists and turns, all of which must be figured into the calculations in order to arrive at an ultimate quantification. But by asking that simple question initially—"How did you hear of us?"—it is possible to trace the path, at the end of which lies ROI quantification.

Asking this one question yields valuable market research, by the way, rather than a precise measure of whether a thoughtleading action of and by itself "works" or "doesn't work." The obstacles to determining the answer to that seemingly simple equation can be great enough for the answer to lie hidden for eons until some detective work helps root it out. For example, a thoughtleading strategy, like any other strategy, can be effective only if it is aimed at the right target market. Is shooting an arrow with a bow more effective at hitting the center of Target A than using a crossbow or even throwing the arrow with your hand? The answer has everything to do with where the arrow is aimed. All three techniques must aim the arrow at Target A's bull's-eye, right? But suppose the arrow, regardless of the technique, were aimed at Target B, which is standing way off to the left of Target A. How likely is it that the arrow will reach the bull's-eye of Target A?

Of course that's silly, you say. Why would any archer do that? Of course you would aim your arrows at Target A!

In business, however, we frequently do not act so logically. We create a product or service that is best suited for a certain target market (Target A), but nonetheless we aim our business development efforts in another direction, at Target B or even Target C or D. This may be because we haven't done any real market research; we have not discovered which target is Target A. We see a number of targets out there and simply guess which one might be the target we should be aiming for. Then we jump up and start fitting arrows to our bow and frantically firing away! When none of our arrows land on Target A, we decide that using a bow and arrow doesn't work. Its ROI, after all, is zero!

I frequently go out and speak, pro bono, to audiences of unemployed job seekers on the topic "Publishing Articles as a Job Search Tactic." I feel strongly that if job seekers got their ideas published, for the purpose of giving them high credibility as specialists in their field as well as for the resulting increased media exposure, they could benefit from this strategy just as surely as do business experts and companies. Before long, they would have employers coming to them, seeking them out, and wondering if they could afford to hire them given their obvious value and, quite possibly, higher salary demands. So I offer myself for free to such groups with the intent of spreading this message.

Another reason I do this, however, a less selfless one, is to utilize the speakers' platform to practice and improve my public speaking skills. I know that when I speak in front of these groups, I can experiment with jokes or with expressing new ideas without risking that I have anything at stake. If I blow a line or if a section of my talk is not received well, I am not going to lose any potential business.

Why do I assume this? Because I learned long ago, after many such speaking appearances, that unemployed professionals are simply not in the proper frame of mind to spend any money at all on a service like mine, even if a good case could be made that the service might help them. The overwhelming majority of jobless job hunters are simply too worried about diminishing whatever resources they currently have, legitimately afraid of reducing their reserves at a time when no replenishments are in sight to rebuild them.

On the other hand, I also speak quite regularly, and frequently pro bono here too, to groups of entrepreneurial professional services providers on basically the same topic, that is, "Publishing Articles as a Business Development Strategy." I *routinely* pick up new clients from these audiences, as entrepreneurs tend to immediately recognize the value of paying for my consulting services if doing so would help them get their ideas published and publicized. They see hiring my firm as a necessary cost of doing business. "You have to spend money to make money," goes the wise old adage.

So ROI can be precisely measured with both audiences and target markets. For the entrepreneur targets, it may be quite high for me. For the jobless job seekers, it's likely to stall at zero. This is true even though at first glance I might think, "These job seekers could really use my services, so they're a good target market for me." Therefore, if thoughtleading is my business development bow and arrow, which target I aim at makes all the difference in terms of achieving a satisfactory ROI, and for shaping my outlook as to whether thoughtleading in fact actually "works."

Dramatic ROI

Which brings us to one of the most dramatic examples of ROI I can dig up. Frequently, published articles and speaking engagements can lead to a significant, direct, and obvious new client return on investment. Other times, a quirkier route to ROI will transpire. New business does not always come wrapped up in a neat, predictable quid pro quo, that is, first a published article, then immediately after … voila! … new clients showing up by phone and e-mail who all carefully read said published article and then came a' callin'.

Our story begins with speaker placement specialist Steve Markman, president of Markman Speaker Management, specialists in placing business experts as speakers in significant business events. My very introduction to Steve Markman provided a fine example of the quirky-road-to-opportunity syndrome, having come about as a result of his telephoning me out of the blue one day because (1) he himself had published an article in a Boston-area business publication that week, (2) I had published an article in the same issue of this publication, (3) my article was laid out on the page opposite Steve's article, causing him (4) to notice in my bio that ran along with the article that I was a publishing expert. Steve had been wanting to connect with someone with my kind of expertise for a long while but had had no idea where to find such a specialist. Coincidentally, I had been wanting to locate a speaking specialist like Steve but had had no idea where to find someone with *his* specialty. Both of us were interested in finding the other because our respective clienteles had been asking us about each other's service, which was frustrating for both of us since neither knew how to provide it.

Steve and I met soon after and agreed to work together whenever feasible and to refer appropriate prospects to each other for a finder's fee. Within days of our agreement, I followed up with a prospect of mine, a professional services firm that had been on the fence for months about hiring me. At this point I was merely checking in with the firm to see if it had made a decision, but it had been indecisive for so long that at this point I felt that the likelihood of ever doing business with the firm was nil. My contact there, Anne, was as pleasant and chatty as always, but was still noncommittal about any decision in my favor as yet.

Then she asked, idly curious, nothing more, "So what's been going on with you lately?"

"Well, I just hooked up with a speaker placement specialist who will now be available to provide speaking services to my clients," I replied, just being chatty, not thinking my response had any particular import.

Yet immediately I could sense Anne's whole demeanor shift across the phone lines. "Really?" she replied. "Hmmm, that's very interesting."

She proceeded to tell me that in fact her firm was planning to bring in a few PR companies to make their pitch about how they could offer the firm PR services that would transform the firm's attorneys into thoughtleaders. "One reservation about your services," she confessed, "has been the perception that you're too limited. The firm does want its associates to publish articles, but it also wants speaking engagements and media services. It's looking for a vendor that can offer all three."

The fact that I could now offer two out of three reenergized the firm's interest in me. Anne had been my inside champion all along, but now I could see that her advocacy had been hampered by my more limited services. That had now all changed.

"And I do have a media PR component too," I added, which was true but was something that we had never discussed because I hadn't known it was important. So to ensure that the firm would let me compete for its business, I brought my PR specialist, Henry Stimpson, into the picture.

When the dust settled after all the interviews with us candidates were over, Steve, Henry, and I had won the business. We had beaten two major Boston-area PR firms, one of them a veritable PR giant, because our combined service was genuinely the one this firm really wanted—a PR focus that emphasized publishing bylined articles and public speaking, thus positioning its practitioners as thoughtleaders. Our competitors took a more conventional approach, offering primarily the development of press releases and the occasional quote or mention in a news story or feature article.

You can see from this incident that I would never have been able to win over this prospect had I not hooked up with both Henry and Steve. Nor would they have won this business on their own either, had they known about the opportunity. And I should add at this point that I initially had met Henry the same way I met Steve: he too had published an article in a Boston-area business publication, and in that case I had been the one to place a phone call and set up a get-together. That meeting too resulted in an agreement between Henry and me to work together.

This development occurred in 2002, and my firm is still serving this particular professional services client today. So how does all this relate to ROI? How can I compute an ROI for that initial article that I published and that Steve saw? How can Steve and Henry compute an ROI for their own published articles?

Well, it took me about two hours tops to write that 800-word article, so if I give myself $250 per hour for writing it (and believe me, I'd better be the one to pay myself this because the publication sure didn't!), then I invested $500 of my time. But the amount of fees that have come my way since landing this client have easily reached well into six figures so far . . . and still counting! When I also throw into the calculations payments from other clients I have landed as a result of referrals or word of mouth from my partnership with Henry and Steve, plus our work with this firm, a conservative ROI could climb above 36,000 percent!

Does this mean that publishing an 800-word article will automatically yield a 36,000 percent return? Of course not, although you can see how it *could*. I can also tell you many other tales of where my $500 investment in writing an article for publication yielded nothing at all. The point is that many factors must be considered when attempting to quantify thoughtleading's ROI, but after all is said and done, if you want to believe, as I do, that practicing thoughtleading pays off, there are plenty of facts, figures, studies, anecdotes, and personal experiences to back you up.

3

Are Thoughtleaders Made or Born?

Destiny is a matter of choice, not chance. It is not a thing to be waited for but to be achieved.

WILLIAM JENNINGS BRYAN

NOW COMES THE MATTER of whether thoughtleaders are born or made. Can one actually become a thoughtleader just by practicing thoughtleading? Or must one have certain innate qualities? Could you be among the unlucky ones whose personal makeup will prevent you from ever joining the ranks of successful thoughtleaders?

As we noted in Chapter 1, Donald Trump, Tom Peters, and others were able to build on their expertise and situations to position themselves as well-known and popular thoughtleading megastars. Then Chapter 2 outlined many good reasons for doing so. But now the question that hangs out for the rest of us is this: Are these folks simply natural-born thoughtleaders? Was there something ingrained in them from birth that has carried them forward and upward to such a degree that they ended up as experts with an unbeatable edge?

Or can thoughtleading be initiated, developed, and nurtured? Can one become a thoughtleader by design? Can one set a goal of becoming a thoughtleader and work at it step by step, literally making it happen?

THOUGHT NOTES

How to Win *Two* Nobel Prizes

Linus Pauling knew the answer to this question. After winning the prize the first time for his pioneering work in the application of quantum mechanics to chemistry, Pauling decided that once was not enough. When asked how you follow winning a Nobel Prize, Pauling famously remarked, "You change careers, of course!"

And so he did. To regenerate his motivation and enthusiasm, he found himself a brand-new mission: world peace! After years of struggle and hard work, he did it again: he won a second Nobel Prize, this time the coveted Nobel Peace Prize.

Had Pauling been destined from birth to become a thoughtleader in these two fields? Unlikely. A more plausible explanation may be his willingness to bear down again and think and act like a thoughtleader one more time. Had it been possible for his life to last twice as long (he died at age 93), perhaps he'd have won a few more. By setting his sights in a new thoughtleading direction despite his advanced age (53) and total lack of expertise in the new field, Pauling showed what should be obvious by now: thoughtleaders are made, not born. They do what needs to be done to get there.

Answers to this question get into the age-old debate of nature vs. nurture, particularly with regard to the origins of high achievers. A thoughtleader in his own right, Dr. Charles Garfield has been studying this issue since the 1970s and has drawn a decided conclusion. Nurture is king, he says. High achievers, whether you call them thoughtleaders or experts or "peak performers" (Garfield's term), are made, not born.

Originally an engineer with the Apollo Space Program, Garfield first conceived the idea of studying peak performers after observing an intriguing and curious dynamic that began just after the first Americans landed on the moon. Up to that point, he says, the motivation to beat the Soviet Union in the race for space had been palpable, day in and day out, at the Kennedy Space Center. Since the day JFK had first declared the dual mission of America's putting a man on the moon "in this decade" and at the same time beating the Soviets there, every fiber of every NASA employee's being seemed hell-bent on achieving these goals. "Peak performers were breaking out all over the place during those years," Garfield recalls.

But unexpectedly, after both goals were achieved, the rarefied air of high achievement melted away. Day-to-day operational tasks slowed down to a humdrum crawl. Mistakes started showing up; deadlines were missed; little of extraordinary merit characterized these days. That special collective mindset of stretching to do the impossible, so predominant up to 1969, no longer reigned. Peak performances seemed fewer and much farther between.

This raised Garfield's interest in the topic. Why had the peak performers who had dominated the NASA culture during the race for the moon seemed to die away once the moon landing took place? To study this in depth, Garfield quit NASA and began his research, ultimately writing a book based on his findings called *Peak Performers*. Its solid conclusion: the excitement and challenge of Kennedy's gauntlet had made all the difference. The thousands upon thousands of space program workers considered themselves involved in something very special and rose to the occasion. What otherwise could have been just another day job had been transformed into something special and historic. In pursuit of such a prize, nearly everyone involved achieved great things, or attempted to.

This ability in all of us to pump ourselves up from mediocrity to greatness can even extend to physiological achievements, Garfield adds. To illustrate, he recounts the story of Roger Bannister, the first speed runner to break the human "barrier" of the four-minute mile. Up until he did so, in 1954, Garfield explains, medical textbooks had insisted that this couldn't be done. Humans were not physiologically capable of running a mile in under four minutes, all the experts said. Although some had come close, within 5 or 10 seconds, no one had actually done it, and so the prevailing thinking of the time was that no one ever would.

Then one balmy afternoon, Bannister, ironically enough a medical student, ran a full mile in 3:59.4. The world was astonished! Along with the acclaim came the feeling that a runner of superhuman proportions was in our midst. Surely we would never witness another human performance like this one again.

"But you want to know what the real miracle was?" Garfield recalls. "Within the next few years, 50 more runners did the same thing." The fact of Roger Bannister's showing the world that breaking the four-minute mile was humanly possible spurred many more runners to push themselves harder, stronger, faster, in the belief—or, more accurately, the knowledge—that the four-minute mile was no longer an impossible dream but something that they could attain if only they worked at it.

"So are peak performers made or born?" Garfield asks rhetorically, summing up. "Made," he insists, answering his own question. "All of them."

THOUGHT NOTES

Thoughtleading the Wiki way

Wikipedia answers the question of how one becomes a thoughtleader this way: "Before one takes the first action-able step, a fundamental shift in mindset is needed. Thought leadership requires a spirit of *generosity*, generosity of one's time, intelligence and knowledge. It requires a trust that by being open with what you know, and by sharing your time and knowledge, the world will reward your efforts."

It's thus a common misconception, or maybe an excuse, that established thoughtleaders should be placed on a pedestal, that it's all quite easy for them and impossible for us. Believing that a famous thoughtleader's achievements must have come about without that person's really trying, that there's a magic gene of some sort that you and I don't possess, contradicts reality. Many successful and famous thoughtleaders would heartily agree, recounting their own hard struggles on their way to the top. The honest ones would admit that they didn't always act like a thoughtleader or instinctively think in the way a thoughtleader should. To get there, they had to push themselves up a very steep hill, toiling in anonymity for years before their big break happened. They relate easily to the apocryphal story of the long-struggling actor who one night wins an Oscar, suddenly becomes a house-hold name, and is immediately labeled by the press as an "overnight sensation."

"Sure, I'm an 'overnight sensation,'" the actor might respond. "It only took me 25 years!"

Stephen Covey: Overnight Sensation #1

One real-life example of a thoughtleading overnight sensation is the now giga-famous Stephen Covey, whose first book in 1989, *The Seven Habits of Highly Effective People*, exploded onto the bestseller lists soon after its publication and never looked back. Once such popular acceptance came Covey's way, other thoughtleading opportunities followed, such as keynoting the world's biggest business conferences, adorning the covers of *Fortune, Forbes,* and *BusinessWeek,* and broadcasting his presentations and seminars on PBS. His books on audiotape, his presentations on videos and CDs, his bylined articles and syndicated columns in newspapers and major magazines—all this and more became the normal tenor of his life. Sequels to *The Seven Habits* followed at a regular clip as well: *Principle-Centered Leadership, The Seven Habits of Highly Effective Families, Everyday Greatness,* and (most recently) *The Eighth Habit: From Effectiveness to Greatness.* Webinars, radio interviews, corporate retreats—at this highest of thoughtleading levels, the list of platforms and vehicles can go on and on.

But for decades before all this came about, Covey had labored in relative obscurity. An academic for most of that period, he remembers the precise moment when, at the age of 57, he struck his thoughtleading spark. This moment fits the characteristic of the true thoughtleader in that had he not been open to new, insightful, and challenging ideas, he might have passed it by. Covey recalls the moment this way:

> *Some years before writing* The Seven Habits of Highly Effective People, *I took my family on a sabbatical leave from the university at which I was teaching. We lived for a year on the north shore of Oahu, Hawaii, and I spent much of the time writing. It was very beautiful there and conducive to contemplation.*
>
> *After an early morning run on the beach, I would retire to an isolated office next to the cane fields on the outside edge of a college. While wandering the book stacks in the college library one day, I noticed a book that piqued my interest.*

Looking through it, my eyes fell upon a paragraph, which powerfully influenced the rest of my life. I read it over and over.

The paragraph communicated the simple idea that there is a space between any stimulus and the response to it. The key to our growth and happiness is how we use that space. The idea hit me with fresh, unbelievable force. It was like an inward revolution. I reflected on it again and again. It was as if I had become an observer of my own participation. I began to stand in that space and look out at the stimuli. It would change my life and the way I communicated forever.

THOUGHT NOTES

Think It Through

To be successful, thought leadership needs to be thought through. In a crowded market, firms need to see who's saying what before they start publishing material. While you may, indeed, have something new to say, you're going to find it harder to get your point across if clients have already heard an awful lot from your competitors. Look for the topics or angles others haven't spotted—the white space.

—Fiona Czerniawska, author of "White Space 2007,"
a unique research report that evaluates the latest
ideas on thoughtleadership published
by the top global consulting firms

Ironically, this "space" that Covey was discovering aptly illustrates the notion of thoughtleaders as primarily made, not born. As Covey explains on his Web site, he chose to pay attention to this new idea. Moreover, he "read it over and over," then from there, bit by bit, he began watering this idea, feeding it, and encouraging it to grow and then bloom until he had built an entire philosophy around it. His resulting seven habits would give birth to his sudden status as an important thoughtleader. But his willingness to open himself up to sudden insight and build upon it, then leap into the abyss of risk by talking about it to others, writing about it, and promoting it, is the essence of a thoughtleader. Thus, if we are capable of learning and making decisions and taking risks, and we all are (yes, all of us), then practicing thoughtleading becomes available to us as well.

Tom Hopkins: Overnight Sensation #2

Exhibit 2 of the capacity of an otherwise nonthoughtleading individual to turn his behavior around and find himself an overnight sensation can be found in the person of Tom Hopkins, a thoughtleader whose insights and teachings in the sales arena have earned him millions of grateful fans and protégés. Tom's first book, *How to Master the Art of Selling*, published in 1980, has since sold over 1½ million copies and has been translated into 10 languages. Used as a textbook in many sales and marketing classes, it's required reading at many companies, too. As was true of Stephen Covey, the success of Tom Hopkins's book quickly sped him forward on the thoughtleader highway, so that before long he was delivering presentations in person to hundreds of worldwide business and sales conferences every year, and via audiotapes and videos to thousands of companies a year and to literally millions of individual sales professionals. His catchphrase, "Training for Champions," has been invoked in the sales departments of companies in every industry.

But Hopkins tells sordid tales of his early sales career in the initial chapters of his first book, about his fumbling sales ability and his elusive success. Selling was simply not something he was very good at when he began his career; in fact, he was so bad at this skill set that one of his early bosses fired him for lacking any discernible selling talent!

Eventually Hopkins surmounted this discouraging assessment by applying himself to the task at hand. He devoted his attention to learning all he could about successful selling by reading, by observing, by experimenting, by practicing, by internalizing, and finally by refining, refining, refining all the various selling techniques he had acquired or conceived. Eventually, his selling results were spectacular. Putting his story and his personally developed sales notions into a book led him to thoughtleading's door, so that now, years after his first book made waves, he continues to write and publish follow-on books covering a variety of topics related to business selling as well as business and life success: *How to Master the Art of Real Estate Sales, Sales Prospecting for Dummies, Sales Closing for Dummies, The Official Guide to Success,* and *How to Make Your Dreams Come True.* Hopkins also conducts live sales training and sales boot camps so that those who want to deeply understand what he has come to know so well can benefit from his direct knowledge and life experiences.

So Tom Hopkins shows that by *practicing* thoughtleading, just like practicing anything, you can attain a high level of expertise at something that in the beginning may not have come very easily. To grasp this, think of something you currently do well:

- Do you play a musical instrument? Practice got you there and keeps you improving.
- Do you ski, snowboard, swim, or play soccer? Practice got you there and keeps you improving.
- Can you type with all 10 fingers? Practice got you there and keeps you improving.
- Do you drive a car? Practice got you there and keeps you improving.
- Do you serve your clients well? Practice got you there too and keeps you improving.

Virtually anything involving a skill or expertise requires hours of practice just to reach a level of basic competence. Thoughtleading is no different. Without practice, all the natural thoughtleading skills that you may have been born with mean nothing. If you are a naturally great writer, but you never write or submit your work for publication, you will not attain thoughtleadership. If you are an eloquent speaker and think fast on your feet, yet you never volunteer to speak in front of groups, you will not attain thoughtleadership. If you are good at conducting interviews and surveys, but you never bother to initiate a study, you will not attain thoughtleadership.

Remember, thoughtleading is both an adjective and a *verb*. Practice will get you there.

The Ballad of Suze Orman

Try this thoughtleading résumé on for size:

> Suze Orman has written five consecutive *New York Times* bestsellers:
> - *Women and Money: Owning the Power to Control Your Destiny*
> - *The Money Book for the Young, Fabulous and Broke*
> - *The Laws of Money; The Lessons of Life*
> - *The Road to Wealth: The Courage to Be Rich*
> - *The Nine Steps to Financial Freedom*
>
> Suze Orman has also written two other books, both national bestsellers:
> - *Suze Orman's Financial Guidebook*
> - *You've Earned It, Don't Lose It*
>
> Suze Orman has won two Emmy awards.
>
> Suze Orman writes a syndicated newspaper column called "Women & Money."
>
> Suze Orman has written, coproduced, and hosted PBS specials based on her bestselling books and, because of her programs' viewership levels during fund-raising periods, has been labeled "the single most successful fund-raiser in the history of public television."
>
> Suze Orman is a contributing editor to *Oprah* magazine.
>
> Suze Orman writes a biweekly column called "Money Matters" on Yahoo! Finance.

Suze Orman writes a bimonthly column for the Costco
Connection.

Suze Orman hosts her own weekly television program on
CNBC.

Suze Orman hosts the *Financial Freedom Hour* on QVC
television.

Suze Orman has been honored with three American Women in
Radio and Television (AWRT) Gracie Allen Awards.

Suze Orman has been inducted into the Books for a Better Life
Award Hall of Fame.

Suze Orman has been honored with a special award in her
name, the Suze Orman First Book Award, which the
Books for a Better Life Award Hall of Fame uses to honor
first-time authors of self-improvement books.

Suze (it's time to drop her last name, since we are getting to
know her so well) was the inaugural recipient of the MS
Spirit Award, recognizing her support of the Multiple
Sclerosis Society over the past five years toward finding a
cure for this disease.

Suze received a 2003 Crossing Borders Award, given by the
feminist press to recognize distinguished women who not
only have excelled in remarkable careers but have also
shown great courage, vision, and conviction, blazing new
trails for women in their fields.

Suze was selected in 2002 for a TJFR Group News Luminaries
Award, honoring lifetime achievement in business
journalism.

Suze has been the keynote speaker at major gatherings all over
the world, from business conventions to conferences for
nonprofits.

Suze is a Certified Financial Planner and at one time served as
vice president of investments for Prudential Bache
Securities and, before that, as an account executive at
Merrill Lynch.

So how does she do it? Surely thoughtleading with such a stellar, consistent, year-after-year record could not have been developed or learned. Suze must have been a thoughtleader from the get-go. How else can we explain all these spectacular thoughtleading results?

Well, take her résumé back one more notch and see what you find: prior to her Merrill Lynch stint, Suze was a waitress at the Buttercup Bakery in Berkeley, California, for seven years!

What changed? What transformed her from a low-level service worker to one of the world's most renowned go-to authorities that millions of people turn to every time?

The truth is that even before her Buttercup years, Suze Orman had had exceedingly lean times with no promise whatsoever of thoughtleader status. Growing up in Chicago, she had dropped out of the University of Illinois in her senior year, purchased a beat-up van with a friend, and hightailed it to California with only a few bucks in her pockets. Despite no prospects at all for either a job or a place to live, the two wanderers found themselves on a back road in the Berkeley Hills, where they encountered a roadblock caused by some workers cutting down trees. Hopping out of the van and striking up a chat with one of the loggers, Suze asked if they might be looking for extra help. Within minutes, she and her friend had tree-clearing jobs at $3.50 an hour. The two young women kept the jobs for weeks, sleeping each night in their van.

Months later, Suze landed the Buttercup job. Years went by, and she got the idea of opening her own restaurant. But her problem was classic: no money! One day, a regular customer, Fred, asked the usually cheery Suze, "Why so glum today?" She explained that she had asked her parents the night before if they could lend her $20,000 so that she could get her business started, but her parents had said no, they didn't feel they could afford to help.

By now a popular waitress at the Buttercup, Suze had earned the respect of many of its customers over the years, but just how much respect she had earned was something that was about to be displayed. The regulars had begun chatting among themselves in an unusual way, and Fred was even going from table to table, asking them to write something.

The next thing Suze knew, Fred was handing her a note and what looked like a stack of personal checks. The note read: "This is for people like you, so that their dreams can come true. To be paid back in 10 years, if you can, with no interest." The checks and IOUs totaled $50,000.

This expression of faith and gratitude by relative strangers stunned her. Possibly more bewildering was that she hadn't a clue as to what to do next. Fred gave her some good advice. "Take these checks to Merrill Lynch tomorrow," he said. "Put them in a money market account, where they can be invested and where this money will grow until you've raised enough to open up your restaurant."

If life came in a neat package, Suze's story would end there. With her natural thoughtleading wisdom and her superhuman instincts for investing and managing money, our story would culminate in her investing the $50,000 and managing to make it grow and grow, capping her success with the opening of a palatial, magnificent restaurant in the East Bay.

But that's not what happened. In fact, Suze's first response to Fred was, "What is Merrill Lynch, and what is a money market account?"

Suze Orman did indeed visit the Oakland office of Merrill Lynch the next day and did indeed commit her new funds to Merrill Lynch's care. But an unscrupulous ML agent got her to sign a paper that allowed him to do exactly what she had told him she couldn't afford to have happen: lose her money. Naively, she trusted him. Within three months, all these restaurant regulars' contributions were gone. Every one of them.

Suze Orman, a naturally gifted financial thoughtleader? Apparently not.

The final chapter of her story finds Suze applying to Merrill Lynch for a job herself, with the attitude, "Well, if they could lose all my money, how much worse could I be at this? I guess the definition of a 'broker' is someone who just makes people broker!" But over time she actually did well, not so much because of her natural instincts as due to her willingness to observe, study, learn, practice, try, risk, fail, succeed—and grow her expertise.

Thought Notes

Collaborate and Question

A thoughtleader is someone who is an astute observer and uses all his other senses to watch for patterns and help shape a new branch of knowledge. To be specific, a thoughtleader is someone who knows how to collaborate with others and to look at a problem from different points of view, and to ask great questions.

—Jim Masciarelli, author of *PowerSkills: Building Top Level Relationships for Bottom Line Results*

Suze also decided, after three months, to do something that most people would consider crazy. To recoup her losses from what that unscrupulous agent had done to her, she sued her employer! But crazy risks sometimes pay off: unbeknownst to her when she filed this lawsuit, the very act of her filing it made her job completely secure. Legally, she couldn't be fired while the lawsuit was in process. And when the lawsuit was finally resolved, via a settlement in which Merrill Lynch agreed to pay back all the money the broker had lost, she was able to return every cent she owed to those kind and generous customers back at the Buttercup.

As Stephen Covey had done, she eventually put her thoughts about how to succeed in business in writing, in her case how to manage one's money, advice that she crafted in particular for women. Her past naiveté and the experience of being taken advantage of because of it helped her build her unique overview. She decided that women by and large are not adequately educated to spot such scams, lacking confidence as well as knowledge when it comes to matters financial. Before long, her thoughtleader focus sharpened and she became an advocate who teaches women how to both hold onto their money and make it grow.

But without her earlier failures and misadventures, Suze Orman would probably never have attained a place in the thoughtleading pantheon. Misfortune gave her an opportunity to learn and grow, and she took advantage of it. She has since been called by *USA Today* "a one-woman financial-advice powerhouse" and by *Worth* magazine a thoughtleader who has "revolutionized the way America thinks about money." Clearly she was not born that way. Despite obstacles in the road, literally (like those logs in the Berkeley Hills) and otherwise, she *made* it all happen.

4

Gauging Your
Thoughtleading Potential

If you're too scared to use your powers, you don't deserve
to have them.

—HIRO, OF THE TV PROGRAM *HEROES*

IS IT TIME TO FIND OUT if you indeed are thoughtleader material?
Maybe you're a thoughtleader already and don't know it. Or maybe you
do know it, or suspect it, but could use some validation. Finally, despite
what we've said about thoughtleaders being made, not born, do you
still secretly fear that perhaps you're not up to the task?

To some extent, we are all thoughtleaders on some level. If you
are an expert on anything at all (engineering, human resources, management, Chinese history, bartending, roofing), you are at least on the
launchpad. You see, all thoughtleaders are experts, although not all
experts are thoughtleaders. Thoughtleaders are experts who have made

a commitment to optimizing their expertise—to fine-tuning their expert's edge. But if you haven't gotten that far yet, you should at least know that if anyone is lauding you, or paying you, for your skills or knowledge or expertise, you have met the basic entry requirements.

A Starbucks barista, for example, who is expert at concocting everything from venti-cinnamon-dolce-lattes to grande-lite-chai-tea-tall-doppio-half-soy-mochaccinos doesn't necessarily know any more than the barista who replaces her on the next shift, so in that sense the two baristas are both experts. But if she wishes to become a barista thoughtleader, distinguishing herself from her shift predecessors and shift successors, not to mention all the many thousands of other baristas out there at all the many thousands upon thousands of Starbucks in the world, she can embark upon a personal thoughtleading strategy to get herself there.

Perhaps understanding the principal characteristics of thoughtleaders would help here. Often the only thing holding a would-be thoughtleader back is an array of misconceptions about what a thoughtleader is and is not. Such misconceptions feed into the thoughtleader wannabe's low self-image, amounting to what I call "thoughtleader jitters."

For example, it's often assumed that a thoughtleader is someone whose ideas are totally original. Well, yes and no. While a thoughtleader's mind should be open to new insights and lessons learned, these insights and lessons may be new to the thoughtleading individual but not new to the world in the strictest sense of the word. They may, however, be new to many of the people who read this thoughtleader's article or book. The old saying, "There's nothing new under the sun" does apply here. Yet 99 percent of the "old" stuff must continually come out again and again, as there will be many younger folk, for example, who have never heard any of it before.

So in case your own misconceptions have created thoughtleader jitters that have been holding you back, here's a "Thoughtleading Inventory" composed of seven questions and commentaries designed to help you gauge your personal and professional thoughtleading potential. Perhaps this inventory can put your jitters to rest and get you off your thoughtleader launchpad.

1. Are You an Entrepreneurial Personality?

You probably are if you are reading this book. Thoughtleading is all about trying something new, and this book permits you to investigate how a thoughtleading strategy might engender in you the expert's edge. Diving deep into the subject of thoughtleading suggests a learning personality, a prime characteristic of entrepreneurialism.

And although the term *entrepreneurs* is typically associated with people who own and run their own businesses, you can also be an entrepreneur within the structure of a firm that you do not own, but that instead employs you. Traditionally such people have been called "intrapreneurs," but they can go by other names as well, such as "corporate entrepreneurs." Susan Foley, managing partner of Corporate Entrepreneurs LLC, writing in her book *Entrepreneurs Inside: Accelerating Business Growth with Corporate Entrepreneurs* (Xlibris), describes the corporate entrepreneurial personality this way:

> *Corporate entrepreneurs are independent thinkers that are looking for meaning at work. They see corporate entrepreneurship as a way to test their skills, flex their muscle and push the edge of the envelope. Corporate entrepreneurs strongly believe in what they are doing and are focused on the end goal. They are creative and find innovative ways to solve problems. They are the creators, doers and implementers that make things happen.*
>
> *Corporate entrepreneurs are dedicated to the project and loyal to the team. They recognize the value of diversity, commitment and trust. They work effectively as an individual contributor and team member. They may not like everyone but they respect them for their contribution. They collectively create a new entrepreneurial culture inside the existing organization. . . .*
>
> *Corporate entrepreneurs are [also] creative. They are motivated and energized when creating and building something new. They are the early adopters of ideas. They see ideas*

not for what they are but what they can become. Corporate entrepreneurs are individual contributors that are interested in creating value and moving the company forward. As a result they gravitate toward those projects at the beginning of the business development lifecycle.

The key to unleashing your entrepreneurial side in your quest to become a thoughtleader, as even the corporate entrepreneurial personality displays, is for you is to eliminate whatever personal "blocks" might be getting in the way of allowing you to think deeply, think creatively, trust and have faith, develop interesting ideas, and firmly commit to a breakthrough result.

If, for example, your response is this: "Yes, it all sounds good, but I just don't have the time," you may be trapping yourself with so many day-to-day operational details that you will never carve out even small amounts of time to experiment and follow through with thoughtleading actions. If that's you, you need to make a promise to yourself to spend X hours a day or X days a week undertaking thoughtleading adventures. Obviously, this book is a fabulous starting place.

But you can't let it end here. Dr. Robert S. Litwak, the former chief of cardiothoracic surgery at Mt. Sinai Medical Center in New York City, recalls that in his days as a resident, despite the round-the-clock shifts that hospital resident doctors were required to endure in those days, he used to grant himself one hour every 24 hours in which he could study and learn whatever he wanted. That usually meant holing up in the hospital library and allowing himself to read purely for curiosity and pleasure. He recalls a mantra that helped him keep this promise to himself: "That's 23 hours for the hospital and 1 for Bob!"

So declare your own hour or two of free time every day so that you too can pursue what you choose. Use the time to develop your thoughtleading self. Stop telling yourself that you don't have the time.

2. Do You Enjoy Finding Creative Solutions to Problems?

When you work with your clients, do you ever run up against a particularly vexing problem? Do you find yourself digging deeper for a solution or developing a new process for resolving a problem? Do you sometimes come up with a completely unexpected happy result?

Are you pleased with yourself when this happens? Does it reinforce your commitment to provide such extra-mile service to your customers?

If so, creativity is in your blood. Creativity is a prime ingredient in thoughtleading. As mentioned earlier, one common thoughtleading jitter goes like this: "I don't have a lot of original ideas; my ideas are just rehashes of what others have said before me." Well, maybe, but then again ask yourself this: How extensively have I analyzed the actual work I do for my clients? Am I discounting the original solutions that I come up with every day, failing to recognize them as creative? Could these everyday solutions of mine be packaged as thoughtleading concepts that are unique to me, and me alone?

Let's say you're a sales expert who has just written an article about sales closing techniques. The actual techniques you describe may not in and of themselves be terribly different from those described in countless books and articles before yours, but what about the examples you use to support your article? If they are drawn from your client files or if they depict ways of using closing techniques that have been personalized and tested by you, could they then be considered unique and original?

By sharing individualized expressions of concepts that have been thought up and written about before, you can rightfully claim ownership of "creative" solutions. That puts you squarely in a thoughtleading frame of mind.

3. Are You Interested in Writing and Publishing an Article or a Book?

The question here is not whether you have written and published anything or whether you would be willing to do so, but rather whether you have any interest in doing so. Because to achieve their expert's edge, genuine thoughtleaders must do this, and do it on a regular basis. To attain this characteristic, it helps enormously if you actually perceive personal benefits from writing. That doesn't necessarily mean that you must find the writing process enjoyable, just that you must see value in the doing of it.

- Would writing an article or a book help you clarify your thinking? Veteran thoughtleaders report that it does.
- Would writing an article or a book provide additional insight into your stated expertise? Veteran thoughtleaders report that it does.
- Would writing an article or a book help you think faster on your feet when making your case to your prospects or when speaking to a group about your ideas? Veteran thoughtleaders report that it does.

But thoughtleader jitters often get in the way of this one, too. In this case, the jitters sound like this:

- I am not a good writer.
- I don't like to write.
- I tried writing an article once and it got rejected.
- I once published an article and nothing happened.

All of these statements may be true, but none of them justifies a decision not to publish. Taken individually, here's how I'd respond:

- I am not a good writer.
  - It doesn't matter. You are an expert; you know things; you have content to offer; you can provide the substance of a

good article. Editors out there are hoping every day that you will pitch them an article idea based on your expert knowledge; if necessary, they will even work with you to shape up your writing. Most likely you'll discover that your writing is not as bad as you have been thinking it is. Once you're over that hurdle, you'll be writing prolifically, no longer self-conscious.

- I don't like to write.
  - It doesn't matter. Do it anyway. Hate every second of it if you must, but do it anyway. Thoughtleading is for grown-ups—it's time to face up to your challenges and responsibilities. They don't give fame and fortune away, you know! Besides, after writing a few pieces and getting them published, you'll most likely discover that this jitter is closely related to the first one (I am not a good writer). You probably just think you don't like to write because you're afraid to face the possibility that your writing is so bad that it will be rejected. Odds are that won't happen.
- I tried writing an article once and it got rejected.
  - So what? Did you submit it to a second, third, and fourth publication? Had you made sure before you submitted it that the publication actually prints articles by outsiders, and not just by members of its own staff? Had you made sure that your article's length (word count) would fit the space requirements this publication has established for an article like yours?

It's a pretty good bet that you answered no to at least one of these questions. Learn the rules of the writing/publishing game so as to set yourself up for success. We'll cover those rules in a later chapter in this book.

- I once published an article and nothing happened.
  - And what exactly were you expecting to have happen? Publishing an article is only a first step; the next is to use your article as a business development tool. Again, know

the rules of the game, in this case the marketing and selling game. This too we'll cover later on in this book. It wasn't the process of publishing an article that went wrong—it was your unrealistic expectations.

4. Do You Have Any Interest in Speaking to Groups about Your Ideas?

As with question 3, the wording of this question is important. Do you have any interest in public speaking? Because again, as a genuine thoughtleader, you must do this.

What thoughtleader jitters get in the way this time? The biggest by far is the abject fear of public speaking itself. Perennially this tops the list of fears mentioned by respondents to surveys about what scares them the most. Fear of death, it is always reported, ranks in second place.

Though fear of public speaking (or is it terror?) might seem like a valid reason for not getting up and doing it, naturally it is not. By being brave and pushing yourself out to speak in public again and again and again, you will make your fear go away, or at least diminish so that it no longer stops you. You will then get better as a speaker and begin to reap the same kinds of rewards as you will with your writing, i.e., you will clarify your thinking, gain additional insight into your expertise, and think faster on your feet.

THOUGHT NOTES

Say It with Gravitas

Being a thoughtleader is to be able to step outside of yourself. You want to have something important to say, something that someone other than you thinks is important. And you want

to have the ability to say it with gravitas. A thoughtleader means owning a predominant share of thought.
—Geoffrey Day, CEO,
The Consulting Exchange

5. Are You Passionate about Your Specialty?

This one's pretty important. Why would you go through all the bother, trouble, sweat equity, and so on if you don't really care about what you're doing and advocating? Without passion, you're not likely to dig deeper to keep learning about your thoughtleading specialty. You're also not likely to try hard to develop original new ideas because it will all feel like just so very much *work*. So make sure you truly care about your area of expertise. If you do not, go find something else.

THOUGHT NOTES

Loving What You Do

I am a specialist in the printer/print buyer relationship—making me an expert in a really narrow field within the commercial printing industry. I'm a 'go-to' authority, a sort of clearing house of knowledge in this one niche. My field is so dry that it elicits guffaws with people outside of the graphic arts, but because I love what I do, it shows, and professionals in the field seek me out looking for all sorts of information, because they see me as a valuable resource. Someone called me a Printing Pundit once—I love that! And professionals in the U.K. have crowned me the "Goddess of Print." It doesn't get any better than that.

> Trustworthiness comes from that, I think, from loving
> what you do. And from an honest willingness too to share info
> about your area. Thoughtleaders are trustworthy and honest.
> There's a lot of integrity involved in being a thoughtleader.
> — Margie Dana, founder, Print Buyers
> International and Boston Print Buyers

6. Are You Willing to Take Risks?

As an entrepreneurial personality (see question 1), you probably have
this one covered. The very essence of entrepreneurialism is risk taking,
so undoubtedly you engage in it frequently. Since you can never be
sure how what you have to say will be received, risk taking is an obvious prerequisite for thoughtleading.

Although you'll certainly develop followers who will agree with
everything you have to say, others will object, argue, disapprove, and
work to prove you are wrong.

Thoughtleader Alan Weiss, author of *Million Dollar Consulting*
(McGraw-Hill) and 24 other books, puts it this way: "Leaders stand
alone. . . . In the Civil War the greatest percentage of casualties among
officers was the brigadier general because he would lead the charge
across the field with his men *behind* him. . . . Real leaders get up on
their horses, yell follow me, then ride off into the line of fire. . . .
Thoughtleaders do that too."

Risk taking, then, is the name of the game.

7. Do You Enjoy Musing about the Future?

Thoughtleaders are valuable to society and to their own businesses
because they muse about the future. The nonthoughtleader, 99 percent of the population, goes bustling about every day keeping day-to-

day things humming. So the other 1 percent has to step back once in a while and consider where all of this is going, or how it could be done differently, hopefully better, or maybe even not at all.

The thoughtleader then lays out a possible scenario, tosses it on the table, and invites the world to take a good look. That's where the "leading" in thoughtleading comes in—the trail blazing, the breaking of new ground.

Sometimes this characteristic results in a whole new way of doing things. Other times such musing falls flat. But the musing itself is essential, and by definition a sublime act, so settle back and enjoy it.

Because if a thoughtleader like you isn't going to do it, who will?

THOUGHT NOTES

Circumspection

Thoughtleading means thinking ahead, and thinking ahead thoughtfully. Not jumping to conclusions about what the future looks like. True thoughtleaders transcend from knowing the answers to seeking the answers. I believe in measuring twice and cutting once. In order to be a thoughtleader, you need to be circumspect about your thinking: the higher the quality, the better your leadership will be.

—Phil Holberton, President,
The Holberton Group

5

Developing Leading-Edge Ideas

The creation of a thousand forests can be found in one acorn.

RALPH WALDO EMERSON

BEFORE YOU EMBARK UPON IT, life as a thoughtleader might sound like a huge commitment of additional time and energy. There's the time involved in researching relevant business topics, drawing conclusions and conceptualizing insights, clarifying your ideas for articles and books, preparing for presentations, and finding time for the media. It would be natural for you to wonder: how in the world can I manage all that? I'm already running flat-out as it is.

The answer is this: it ain't about time, it's about perception. And it's about your ongoing attitude, your mindset, and literally the way you choose to think. True thoughtleading weaves itself into one's moment-to-moment thinking. New ideas arise all of an instant, in the blink of an eye. Yes, a *blink!* You don't necessarily set aside time to think and reflect—although you *could.* Instead, you develop a new mode of thinking that replaces your old way and now serves your thoughtleading objectives, all without any added burden of making more time or being distracted from your daily chores.

Suzanne Lowe, author of *Marketplace Masters: How Professional Service Firms Compete to Win,* puts it this way:

> *Does thoughtleading take too much time? Well, it shouldn't. It's not about time at all. Rather than being time-consuming, thoughtleading should be a constant process . . . small steps, great gains. It's more about an approach to thinking critically. If you simply focus your thinking within a framework of wondering why or how did this or that happen, then you will fix on the substance of a situation and ask critical questions. Thoughtleaders possess an investigator's mind, thinking like a detective moment to moment. It does not have to take any particular extra time at all. In fact, I thought up many of my ideas for my book while walking my dog! Thoughtleading is about employing a different thought process, not just taking more time to think differently at specified times.*

Maria Thomson, author of *Insurance Coverage for All . . . and How Businesses Can Afford to Provide It* (Actex Publications), sees thoughtleading thinking as allowing oneself to simply be curious and wonder about things. To develop the forward-thinking ideas for the insurance industry that she eventually published in her book, she continually focused on the why of things, asking question after question of others as well as of herself.

"For many years I puzzled over a serious industry problem," she recalls. "A number of solutions were tried by companies but none succeeded. I kept pursuing the answers. It was an interesting and absorbing challenge."

Jim Masciarelli, author of *PowerSkills: Building Top-Level Relationships for Bottom-Line Results*, considers thoughtleading thinking to be a powerful mindset. He was initially inspired to become a thoughtleader by a success poster brandishing this line: "Become the most positive and enthusiastic person you know." He translated that to mean that the best thing any of us can do is attempt to "improve our souls on this earth by living, loving, and learning."

"To me that's what it's all about," he says. "The more you learn, the more you can offer other people. Learning is the ultimate elixir. No matter how old you are, learning is what makes you feel alive. Life as a thoughtleader is an antidote for aging."

Can we doubt this when we watch lifetime thoughtleaders, in business and elsewhere, grow older and older, yet never lose their zest? Think of Peter Drucker, who questioned, researched, wrote, and reflected until his death in 2005 at the age of 96.

How about John Kenneth Galbraith, who was still publishing, speaking, and musing until his death in 2006 at the age of 97?

Other examples? Norman Mailer, Studs Terkel, Jack Lalanne, Duke Ellington, Julia Child. No matter what the person's age, the thoughtleading mind keeps on cranking out new thoughts, imagining, reflecting, wondering, questioning—all without missing a beat.

You Literally Have to Lead

Despite all the positive glories of thinking like a thoughtleader, however, there are nonetheless cautions to consider. Maria Thomson recalls, for example, that thoughtleading thinking can leave you standing all alone, possibly too far ahead of your time.

"The original areas that I tried to take a stance on failed to gain acceptance," she recalls. "My thinking on the new directions I was advocating for the insurance industry was too far ahead of where the market was, too far into the future." As a result, her attempts to win business were often rebuffed, with her prospects giving lip service to her progressive ideas but not being willing to back this up with cold hard cash. Only years later did her ideas about using technology to streamline insurance underwriting begin winning favor. Now, five years later, many of her pioneering ideas are mainstays of the insurance industry, even though during her earlier advocacy the prevailing wisdom of the industry doubted that they would ever work.

Courage is thus a prerequisite for thoughtleading thinking. Not only will you develop new ideas on an ongoing basis, but you'll need to communicate them too, put them up for debate, and invite disagreement and denunciation and even derision.

"You literally have to lead," explains Alan Weiss, author of *Million Dollar Consulting* and self-proclaimed contrarian, "and not necessarily because you invent an alternative to gravity or an alternative to teamwork or whatever, but because you help people look at something in a new way. You have to contribute to the state of the art, and to do that you always have to be able and willing to stand out and be recognized in a crowd."

He adds

> *It's not enough for a true thoughtleader to just "think"; real thoughtleading is more than that. I've met a lot of people who are good thinkers, and whom I have learned from . . . but thoughtleadership in any discipline literally means being willing to stand out in a crowd and say, "Here is the right way to do it; now take your best shot." You've got to manifest your thoughtleadership, and you can never use nonoriginal work. It takes chutzpah to put your own ideas across, but that's what thoughtleaders do."*

THOUGHT NOTES

Break It and Remake It

I don't actually like that term "thoughtleader," because to many people, it's simply a way of becoming more visible. But what we really should be talking about is breaking the mold of what has been accepted up until now, reshaping old ways and assumptions into things that are new and innovative. . . . You break it and remake it. Thoughtleading is much deeper than merely gaining more visibility and spreading around your thoughts in broader circles. It's actually about forcing yourself and others to push the envelope.
—Suzanne Lowe, author of *Marketplace Masters: How Professional Service Firms Compete to Win*

Failure Is Desirable

Accepting the idea that thoughtleading means standing up on a platform all by yourself and inviting a roomful of scrutinizers to take potshots at you may require a redefinition of failure. Experts, like all humans, want to do their best and to do things right, do things well, and get recognized for excellence. Succinctly put, they want to win.

Yet sometimes failure *is* winning, paradoxical as that must sound. There are actually many benefits to failing, so the trick is not to feel as if failing is the worst thing that can ever happen. In fact, failure is desirable.

Consider these three potential benefits of failure:

1. Failure can teach you how *not* to do something.

2. Failure can suggest that an opposite or alternative way to do something is the path to success. It may provide an "aha!" for something that had not been previously considered. Such inventions as Post-its and Plexiglas came about because the experiments that created them had originally been designed with other product inventions in mind.

3. Failure can sometimes represent a step along the way to success. No better example comes to mind than Thomas Edison. While searching for the secret to electric light, he failed more than 3,000 different times as he tried out materials for the lightbulb's filament until he inserted tungsten and—poof—there was light! When asked later how it was that he had achieved this miracle when so many others had not, he replied, "Well, I was willing to do what the others would not. Keep failing but refuse to give up."

Failing is an inevitable component of life, one that is impossible to avoid completely. By worrying about it, fearing it, and trying to keep it completely out of your life, you make it more difficult for new ideas or successful outcomes to find their way in. And that's the part that's the real mistake: wanting so badly to never make one.

Alan Weiss likes to say, "If I'm not failing, I'm not trying." Thoughtleaders do fail, and often that's the very thing that leads to their success.

THOUGHT NOTES

Sending Your Book to College

Thoughtleading gets down to metaphysics. We start thinking about ourselves, about what is driving us. Is it our background, our parents? Is it how we envision ourselves? Is it who we are in the present?

Some people practice thoughtleading because they don't want to have another kid. So they mold their thoughts. Thanks to thoughtleadership, they can control their own universe. . . . You look at the big players, they might have 15 children or 15 books. . . .

But then you gotta send your book to "college," i.e., to corporations, to professional groups, to business leaders . . . get it in the hands of other people. It's your baby, your offspring . . . your child!

—Louis Carter, President, Best Practice Institute, and author of *The Change Champion's Fieldguide* and *Best Practices in Leadership Development and Organization Change: How the Best Companies Ensure Meaningful Change and Sustainable Leadership* (Essential Knowledge Resource Publishers)

Tenets of Creativity

As most of my program participants sketched furiously, swirling brightly colored markers across large white sheets of poster paper, my eyes locked on Rhonda, who was kneeling on the floor, motionless, in the middle of the seminar room. Her eyes stared distantly beyond the sheet of paper spread out on the floor in front of her. She looked as if she was refusing to participate. As she'd been somewhat resistant to the creativity process I'd been teaching all day, I worried that she might be refusing to do what I'd asked.

In my seminar called "Unlocking Your Creativity," Rhonda would in fact have appeared to be the last person who would resist. She was, after all, a talented fine artist who was skilled in many media, unlike most of the more logical, "left-brained" management professionals who were attending this program. Why was she unwilling to give the exercise a chance?

When everyone had finished, I asked for volunteers to share their "vision of the future." An accountant named George raised his hand.

"Here's a boat on the ocean," George said, standing and holding up his "vision poster" in which a crude sketch of a boat filled up the paper with himself, a stick figure, as the boat's captain.

"I'd love to retire one day and just sail away!" he said. "I love sailing. A dream life for me would be to get out on the water every day and just feel the breeze."

We asked a few questions, offered encouraging comments, then gave George a round of applause. Marcie got up next, announcing that she'd love to spend more time with her kids. Her self-portrait showed her standing with three small children next to a house, snow-capped mountains, the beach, a general store. "It would be just lovely to spend more time with them than I can right now," she said. "Maybe I could work toward that."

Again, we asked questions, offered encouragement, and acknowledged Marcie with applause. The intent of this exercise was to get all the attendees thinking about what they *wanted* to do, not what they felt they *had* to do. So often we get bogged down in trying to solve problems with our logical minds, searching for "realistic" solutions. In the process, we shut down our creative thinking. Then good ideas for solving our problems and changing our lives stop coming up, and we table our hopes and dreams, mistakenly believing that our problems had no solution.

So the idea here was to express hopes and dreams in unfamiliar media, illustrating them in bright colors, revving up the less-used creative segments of the brain in the hope of stimulating "breakthrough" ideas. Many incidents in history, especially business history, have become legendary for demonstrating that this theory works. Velcro, for example, came about when a Swiss engineer named George de Mestral perceived a connection between the burrs that stuck on his pants when he hiked through the woods and a new way to fasten things. He got to work on making a burrlike material that would catch and fasten in the same way, and Velcro was born.

Similarly, the plate glass industry was revolutionized after Albert Pilkington observed grease forming in the dishwater as he was doing dishes. Something about the image led him to invent a process for making glass, for the first time, perfectly smooth; he called the result Plexiglas.

By now, four or five participants had shared their posters. To my surprise, Rhonda raised a hand to go next, despite the untouched poster paper still stretched out before her on the floor.

"Here's a vision of *my* life," she said, picking up the blank sheet of paper. "It's a clean slate. By leaving the paper blank, I give myself freedom. I want to live my life spontaneously from now on, no more worrying and being 'practical' all the time. I'll draw on the poster and insert things as I go along."

Creative thinking is often referred to as thinking "outside the box," thinking beyond the conditioned boundaries of mental preconceptions. By drawing absolutely nothing on her poster paper, Rhonda, a skilled artist who could have dazzled us with all sorts of brilliant images, drove the lesson home. Ignoring both "shoulds" and "spozedto's," she'd reached a completely different place, stimulating her thinking dramatically and locating the right answer for her.

THOUGHT NOTES

Where Groupthink Begins

When my daughter Chloe was about three, I used to take her to a local kid fitness program called "Toddler Gym." We had tried to give Chloe a fair amount of freedom at home to roam and discover and enjoy, and this program seemed to be set up the same way. The little balance beams and flouncy giant parachute to hide under and the colorful balls of all sizes stimulated her not only physically but creatively.

> But one day, the instructor called all the little kids into a circle for some kind of group game. Chloe, however, was still exploring off to the side, so the instructor called (nicely), "Come on, Chloe, come over and join the circle." At that moment, I thought, "Uh-oh, here it comes. Regimentation. Groupthink. Her days of totally free-rein, unencumbered, independent exploration have come to an end."

Innovations Equal Success

Rick Harriman, chairman of Synectics Inc., based in Cambridge, Massachusetts, one of the world's leading creativity consulting firms, warns that managers who believe that their company can survive in today's climate without ongoing, abundant creative thinking in its ranks are kidding themselves. "It's a very dangerous thing for companies to feel they're sitting pretty the way things are happening today," he explains. "Our clients' perspective is that when you're faced with the kind of continual market and product changes we are seeing today, you've got to get ahead of the curve. That demands utilizing creativity."

Harriman's firm reaches out all over the world to train managers in the art of innovative thinking; in fact, it was the first such firm to do so, some 60 years ago. He says that to stay ahead of the competition today, you must seek out opportunities that were not previously available, which you do by "keeping your mind open and recognizing that, since factors are constantly changing, so must you." He adds, "View change as opportunity, not crisis."

Research conducted by Synectics in which hundreds of senior managers were surveyed identified a correlation between a company's commitment to innovation and its success in the marketplace. The high-performing companies are labeled "Stars." There are also two other categories: "Seekers" and "Spectators."

With success defined as increases in such areas as revenues and profits, employee retention, maintaining high morale, and consistent introduction of high-quality products and services, Stars lead in all categories. The Seekers come next, owing to a modicum of innovation in their cultures, while the steadfastly traditional Spectators trail far behind.

It seems a wise move, then, for a company to inject innovative thinking into its organizational mix. To do this right, creativity experts agree, whether for an organization or an individual, requires four "creativity tenets":

1. *Let ideas fly.* Managers and even colleagues must learn to resist the temptation to blurt out, "No, no, that would never work!" during a meeting, and especially during a brainstorming session. The essence of creativity is to let all ideas fly, no matter how wild, impractical, or outrageous they may be. Even putting totally wacky ideas on a white board for all to see could end up opening the discussion to an ultimately practical solution. No idea should be considered unworthy. Remember Rhonda.

THOUGHT NOTES

First Thought, Best Thought

The Beat poet Allen Ginsberg used to advocate a decision-making process that he called "first thought, best thought." Believing that his best poetry efforts invariably came about when he stuck to his initial thoughts and the way he expressed them, he worked hard to nix his inner, nagging self-doubt in favor of rewriting first drafts only occasionally. Rather than agonizing over the merit of his first concept for a poem, he just went with it, taking his chances that his readers would react to the work favorably. His trust of his inner gut reigned supreme.

2. *Failure is desirable.* Yes, here it comes again. Many companies give lip service to the idea that it's OK to fail, that making mistakes and getting things wrong is par for the course. But then look out if you really do mess up!

   Instead, managers who are committed to innovation will invite open discussion of mistakes and failures on the theory there's always a lesson to be learned from them. After all, by definition, taking risks means that sometimes you win and sometimes you lose. Failure must be understood as only one possible outcome in the overall game.

3. *Color, music, and quiet are vital.* The first things to go when budgets get tight in our schools, it seems, are such "nonessentials" as art and music. Yet many brain studies indicate that creativity is amplified when such traditionally "peripheral" educational activities are included in the curriculum.

   Thus, creative companies find ways to allow music in the work environment, maintain a colorful decor, give employees downtime and space to think, and reimburse employees for programs that allow them to (as Stephen Covey puts it) "sharpen their saw."

4. *Travel roads not traveled.* If a company intends to truly transform itself into one that routinely practices innovation, it must take risks as a culture. That means choosing unknown directions, attempting grand experiments—leaping off cliffs! Step out of your traditional business practices when they seem not to be working and try something unusual, or even wacky.

   In his early days as a sales professional, Josh Gordon, author of *Presentations That Change Minds* (McGraw-Hill), had a terrible time getting one prospect to look at his marketing materials. Each time he made a follow-up call to this prospect, the prospect insisted that he just wasn't interested in Josh's product. So why should he bother to look at Josh's materials?

One day, out of total frustration, Josh decided to try the exact opposite of what he'd learned back in sales training. He stuffed all his marketing materials into a big cardboard box and wrote all over it in crayon warnings like, "Do NOT open this box!" and "Do NOT look inside!" and "Whatever you do, keep this sealed!" Then he mailed the box to his prospect, with no return address.

As this was before September 11, you can imagine what happened: the prospect couldn't help himself; he just *had* to look inside. Once he caught a glimpse of Josh's lively marketing materials, he began to change his mind about Josh's product. Before long he was ringing Josh up and giving him his business. By taking a road rarely traveled — never, in fact! — Josh won new business that would not have been won without his innovative attempt.

Words That Kill Creativity

And now a few utterances that you will *not* hear emanating from a thoughtleader's mouth any time soon:

- "We tried that before."
- "It's a good idea, but we really don't have time to implement it."
- "You're joking, of course."
- "That's all very well in theory, but practically speaking . . . "
- "Top management will never go for it."
- "But we've never it done it that way before."
- "I'm afraid you're ahead of your time."
- "Has anyone else ever tried it?"
- "We should form a committee and study this idea further."

Words That Spark Creativity

And finally, a few words that thoughtleaders *do* like to say:

- "Imagination is more important than knowledge."

  —ALBERT EINSTEIN

- "In the long history of humankind (and animalkind too), those who learned to collaborate and improvise most effectively have prevailed."

  —CHARLES DARWIN

- "There is no such thing as a failed experiment, only those with unexpected outcomes."

  —BUCKMINSTER FULLER

- "If you can dream it, you can do it."

  —WALT DISNEY

- "If you have built castles in the air, your work need not be lost; that is where they should be. Now put the foundations under them."

  —HENRY DAVID THOREAU

- "Think before you speak is criticism's motto; speak before you think, creation's."

  —E. M. FORSTER

- "Think wrongly if you please, but in all cases think for yourself."

  —DORIS LESSING

- "A problem is a chance for you to do your best."

  —DUKE ELLINGTON

- "You see things and say 'Why?' but I see things that never were and say 'Why not?' "

  —GEORGE BERNARD SHAW

6

The Five Pillars
of Thoughtleading

---

*I can give you a six-word formula for success: Think
things through . . . then follow through.*

—Captain Eddie Rickenbacker

Contrary to popular misconceptions, injecting publishing, public
relations (PR), and media attention into your life should *not* consist primarily of sending out press releases and occasionally getting yourself
quoted in an article, or maybe on the radio or cable TV. Yet if you hire
most PR firms or an independent publicity specialist, you'll probably
get opposite advice. Most PR firms specialize in "media hits," which
works out fine if your concept of PR and media is just hiring someone
from the outside and letting them do pretty much everything. When
you do that, you've decided that media is a function that someone takes
care of, rather than something that you and your people or colleagues

get personally involved in. With that attitude, you will never, repeat never, attain your expert's edge.

Thoughtleading requires a more intellect-based approach. The foundation of your expert's edge is inside your head. Your individualized intellectual capital makes you special. There's no one you can outsource this treasure to.

What's needed, then, is to focus on five "pillars" of thoughtleading, five specialized tactical areas that will ensure that your clients and prospects keep turning your way every time. These five pillars are typically either ignored by even the most aggressive PR marketers or executed in too conventional a manner. But with a thoughtleading frame of mind driving each pillar, your overall "visibility campaign" will be transformed.

Here are the five pillars of thoughtleading:

Pillar 1: Publishing your ideas. Bylined articles and books are typically not included in traditional PR, whose practitioners prefer instead to write press releases and cultivate media contacts. And when they do help out with getting articles written and published, the articles tend to be ghostwritten for the client. Books, by the way, are often deemphasized or excluded entirely, being a completely foreign world that is not even remotely understood by the usual PR specialist.

Regarding ghostwriting, my bias is that thoughtleaders do their own writing, even if they believe that they are not good writers. One can always improve. Thoughtleaders must not outsource the hard work of developing and expressing their thoughts, which ghostwriting does by turning the process into a phony exercise. The thoughtleader ends up taking credit for writing an article or a book but secretly hiding the fact that he or she actually did not do so.

Pillar 2: Speaking before groups and followers. Speaking gigs can be hard to come by and fraught with dangerous variables, such as poor audience turnouts, travel nightmares, and disorganized conference planning. So PR folks stay away from them, and perhaps rightfully so. Yet speaking is something that you must do if you are to attain and maximize your expert's edge. Fortunately, when coupled with publishing, especially publishing a book, public speaking eventually takes care of itself, as word gets out that an author is willing and able to come and speak to one's group.

Pillar 3: Keeping your edge with fresh thinking. Thoughtleading requires fresh, vibrant thoughtleading thinking, not just relying on dusty old ideas copied from someone else's speech or book. Original research studies or interviews for a new article or book are the thoughtleader's mainstay for revitalizing assumptions and developing new insights. Conventional PR techniques rarely have much to do with thought origination or renewal.

Pillar 4: Creatively leveraging the Internet. While PR traditionalists certainly use the Internet to spread the word about their clients, as avoiding the Net is growing increasingly impossible, their use of the Net does not always show up as especially innovative. Thoughtleaders instead find and conceive ways to leverage the Web and their e-communications so that the Net's potential is realized and connected directly to their expert's edge.

Pillar 5: Making vigorous use of the media. This may be the thoughtleading pillar that most approximates the practices of conventional PR. However, thoughtleaders attain their expert's edge here in the same manner as with Pillar 4: by tying their thoughtleading actions to media opportunities whenever possible. Their press releases, for example, rather than being the often dry drivel about a company's new product or recent hires, tend to be more often an announcement of a recently published article or a speaking engagement. This makes the expert's content and ideas the focus of the release rather than some mundane operational "news" or even the publishing or speaking event itself. This type of PR is utilized as a *supplement* to the other pillars, a supporting cast member if you will, rather than as the lead pillar or star technique.

With this five-pillar overview in mind, let's turn now to an in-depth focus on the first pillar, publishing your ideas, which is so important and so complex that I have broken it down into two chapters, the first about publishing books, and the second about publishing articles. There is much to say and much to learn, but once you have understood, practiced, and mastered this pillar, 80 percent of your expert's edge will have fallen into place and launched you as a thoughtleader.

7

Pillar 1A: Publishing Books

The greatest single marketing device I've encountered,
after buyer-to-buyer referrals, is publishing.

ALAN WEISS

THE PINNACLE OF THE EXPERT'S EDGE is reached when a thoughtleader writes and publishes books. Though such an endeavor can appear overwhelming to many would-be thoughtleaders, there's no denying a book's many impacts. When you write a book, all the pieces fall into place. You need a ton of research and experience to write a book, which paves the way for finding enough insights and lessons learned to fill your book's pages.

While the same can also be said about writing articles (and in fact, if the prospect of a book looms as too formidable for you, starting instead with writing an article might be your best tack), books allow thoughtleaders to really strut their stuff, delving deep into their thoughtleading knowledge and covering the whole map of their expertise.

A second impact is a book's positive effect on winning speaking engagements, especially at high-level conferences, company retreats, and other major professional events. Authors of books tend to be at the top of the list of desirable speakers for planners of such events, which in turn sometimes attract business and mainstream media. Reporters from both print and online publications who wish to keep their eyes and ears open for new article ideas may end up approaching a speaker, and even bloggers who are eager to identify new concepts to write about will be eager to publicize the expert behind the lectern as well. So by writing and publishing a book, you end up traversing all five thoughtleading pillars at once: publishing, speaking, research, media, and the Internet.

Does this mean that you should just sit down and start writing, stopping only after you've filled a few hundred Word document pages? Not quite. There's a lot to consider once you've made the decision to write and publish a book, so hold onto your quill pen. Let's start at the beginning with the most important initial question: will your book idea advance your business goals?

Thought Notes

A Book Makes You Special

Once I had a book published, when I walked into a room, people seemed to perk up and take notice. I seemed to almost magically have gained greater credibility.

—Bill Roiter, author of *Corporate MVPs: Managing Your Company's Most Valuable Performers* (Wiley)

Advancing Your Goals

As is true with all of our thoughtleading pillars, your first decision must always be lined up with your strategic business objectives. So, given that rule, what should your book be about?

To answer this question, consider these other questions:

- What do you want to be known for?
- What high value do you currently bring to your customers?
- A reputation as an expert in what area would enable you to sell more of your products or services?
- What is it about you and your firm that currently attracts prospective customers?
- What do you want to be known for in the future (in addition to what you are currently known for or what you want to be known for *now*)?

Note that all these questions can apply to an entire organization as well as to each individual in it and to the business expert who works alone. These questions have to do with the thoughtleading image that would best suit a company or individual's business development strategy. To identify the correct image, zero in on what currently defines you and your firm as valuable to customers. What do you typically say at a networking event when you are asked what you do? What would you write if you had to bang out a quick e-mail on the subject? How do you describe reasons for hiring you when delivering a sales presentation?

Your book should reinforce whatever your answers to these questions would be. You don't want to publish just any old book; you want to publish the *right* book. Thus your value proposition must be reinforced and made clear to your readers, any of which is a potential new customer for you or at least a potentially strong word-of-mouth referral source.

Forget this and you end up leaving a trail of missed and broken opportunities. I saw a sterling example of this a few years ago while doing a seminar at an American Management Association conference in Atlanta. On the opening day, I listened to a dynamite keynote speaker who truly captivated not only me but his entire 750-member audience. His presentation was unique, motivating, and energizing, and it left everyone begging for more. When it was over, people rushed outside to the lobby to search the conference bookstore for his book.

After a captivating speech of that nature, attendees want to take home a book as a way of sinking more deeply into the speaker's thinking. The book also represents a kind of "refresher course" months or even years down the road. For the speaker/author, this provides a significant add-on benefit to the day's proceedings: the book functions as a very impressive take-home advertisement that may sit on the buyer's bookshelf or desk for years, all the while promoting the speaker and his or her expertise and business. Each time the book buyer glances toward it, both the presentation and the speaker/ author's value proposition are replayed. The presence of the book also allows a visitor to the book buyer's office to be drawn into the circle of knowledge about the speaker/author. The visitor will also be hearing a ringing endorsement.

As well, a book can point its purchaser to the author's Web site, perhaps leading to the book buyer signing up for the author's e-letter. This may lead to the book buyer's one day becoming a bona fide client. At the very least, the book buyer gets drawn into the speaker/author's "client community," which possibly means that three years down the road a new book is bought and the cycle continues. Sweet loyalty is made of such as this.

So with all this fabulous fallout awaiting this particularly spectacular speaker at this AMA conference in Atlanta, what did I observe that day that I never forgot? What did I take home with me? Sad but true: the speaker did not have a book to sell! He hadn't written one yet; he hadn't published one. I wasn't able to take home any substantive expanded content, just the memory of my frustration. What's worse for the speaker, as a result of there being no book, today, some years later, I can no longer call up the name of that speaker. He had me that day; I was quite an instant fan. But that means nothing if you walk out of the room with nothing to keep the flame alive.

What Kind of Book Could *You* Write?

To advance your reputation as an expert, apply these suggestions to your own expertise and imagine a book that *you* could write, keeping in mind that a special "hook" will be required to set your ideas apart from conventional thinking:

- If you're a sales expert, you could write a book about how to improve one's sales skills or about specific aspects of improving one's sales skills, such as sales prospecting, delivering a sales presentation, and/or sales closing techniques.
- If you're a math professor, you could write a mathematics textbook for a particular grade level, or a book about how math can be integrated into day-to-day living, or a book about the math concepts that give people the most trouble.
- If you're a biotech engineer, you could write a book about stem cell research possibilities, amazing new biotech products on the horizon, or the implications (positive and negative) of biotech developments for society.
- If you're a leadership expert, you could write a book about how to lead a corporate management team effectively, how leadership differs from managing, or how to be an effective leader in a nonprofit or volunteer organization.

And note that you are currently reading my book about how thoughtleading can offer you an "expert's edge." As you learn from me, you are simultaneously learning about my expertise and my company's core services. That's the kind of alignment all your thoughtleading actions should have.

Are You Ready?

Have I convinced you that it would be worth your while to write and publish a book? If I have convinced you of this, then—are you ready?

To be ready means to be prepared to set aside a huge amount of time and emotional energy, coupled with the will to see this through come what may and to get the job done.

For many would-be thoughtleaders, this question is a tough one. Writing and publishing a book is not a commitment that everyone is ready to make. It's akin to every other major life commitment: getting married, having a baby, raising a family, buying a house, studying for a Ph.D., or starting a business. It will take a lot of your time, persistence, reflection, research, organization, and writing. Yes, and writing: writing, writing, writing—and rewriting!

THOUGHT NOTES

Every Day

I worked on my book from 5 to 7 a.m. every day. It was the only time I could do it, what with raising kids and working all-out at the same time. You chip away at it, and at some point you say, 'Wow, I know all that stuff; I've done all that.' You keep working away at it, and eventually you get it done.
—Nancy Stephens, author of *Customer-Focused Selling: Understanding Customer Needs, Building Trust and Delivering Solutions . . . the Smarter Path to Sales Success* (Adams Media)

If you're not ready to tackle a book, that's fine. Feel free to skip to the next chapter, which discusses publishing articles. But if you want to at least learn more about what's involved, stay aboard. Once you know more about how the process works, you might end up changing your mind.

Is Ghostwriting the Easy Answer?

You might presume that one way out of this overwhelming fix would be to hire a ghostwriter. Ah, it smells so right! The ease with which your book will get prepared and written while you go about your regular business; one more task delegated that you don't have to carry out personally. What a simple but beautiful solution.

Well, not so fast! Even with a ghostwriter, you'll need to spend a considerable amount of time educating your "ghost" about your personal knowledge, experiences, message, and insights. You'll also need to review your ghostwriter's drafts, helping to revise them as necessary. You'll need to recognize and correct errors, and reteach your writer aspects of your expert knowledge that he or she hasn't quite gotten. You may even need to help your ghost rewrite some passages so that the wording truly reflects what you'd like to say.

Because of all these duties for which you will still need to be available, my advice is to forget about using a ghostwriter altogether. Even if you loathe the idea of writing anything, or you don't think you are any good at writing, or you wonder where in heck you could ever find the time, I still suggest sucking it all up and attempting to do the writing anyway.

With a good editor, even your roughest drafts will eventually be converted into good, solid, readable prose. If your writing is truly rough or in need of major editing, you'll probably need to hire an editor to help you, as publishing house editors these days have too little time to provide high levels of attention. But no matter what hurdles you have to overcome, when it's all over, you'll have achieved what had initially seemed impossible: you'll have written a book! And you won't have to hide your ghostwriter from your public, pretending that you wrote the thing. You'll be able to proudly and honestly proclaim the book as an achievement of your very own.

Keep in mind that once we make a commitment, however shaky or even terrifying, even when we aren't sure how we will ever achieve such a daunting thing, most of us usually find a way to finish it. Making the commitment by itself sets up a success timeline.

As the great bandleader Duke Ellington once remarked, "I don't need time . . . I need a deadline!" With a deadline, and with a taskmaster as well, say a mentor or coach or editor, something great may magically emerge from an otherwise uncomfortable and unconfident beginning.

THOUGHT NOTES

243 Pages

Publishing my first book greatly increased my stature, something I find highly ironic because in fact all I really did was capture and organize all the things I have been talking and writing about piecemeal (in articles, presentations, and one-on-ones) for many years. Though it does have a ton of original work in it too, it's more the fact that I could actually have enough substance for 243 pages, a packaging that attracts a lot of attention. People react with an "Omigosh!" look in their eye, as in "You've written a book?" There's a catch in their voice. "It was published?" Yes, it was published! This truly impresses people.

—Suzanne Lowe, author of *Marketplace Masters: How Professional Service Firms Compete to Win*

Which Option Is Right for You?

Let's now assume that you have decided to go forward, that you are indeed ready to make the commitment to writing and publishing a book. The next step for you is *not*—I repeat, *not*—to sit down and start writing. You must first choose which publishing option is best suited for you.

For 99 percent of us, the only option that immediately comes to mind is to start looking for a publisher. We assume that this is the best option for a lot of reasons, most of them misconceptions. We hope, for example, that we will locate a "top" publisher based in New York City, because such a publishing house will market, promote, and sell our book for us, sending us out on a media tour of many cities, arranging countless media interviews, and of course putting many thousands of copies of our book out there on the shelves of all the bookstores. Oh, and of course we will be given a substantial "advance" payment of perhaps $40,000, $50,000, or $60,000 so that we will be able to put our business aside and work full time on the book for three to six months. Maybe a distant cousin of yours landed a similar deal, or maybe you've read about such things in the newspaper. That's usually the closest most people come to this particular publishing fantasy.

Misconceptions about Book Publishing

Unfortunately, signing a contract with a commercial book publisher typically does *not* work like this. And that's if you're lucky enough to find a publisher at all, even one that is not in New York City, but instead is perhaps a small firm located in Illinois, California, or Kansas. The fact is that landing a publishing contract at all is a supercompetitive endeavor. To also expect your publisher to set you up with a high-level promotion campaign is not only doubly unlikely but 95 percent of the time totally off the wall.

So before you jump into a dreamy, romantic quest to capture a big-name commercial book publisher, take note of the following misconceptions that most of us carry around in our heads for virtually our whole lives. In terms of what a publisher can and/or is likely to do for you, your understanding of the realities of the book-publishing world will take you a long way toward making or breaking your ultimate book-publishing success:

Misconception 1

A book publisher will aggressively promote me and my book, ensuring my book the widest possible visibility.

Well, in an ideal world, all publishers would *like* to provide this, but in the real world, the scarcity of their own resources typically prevents it. Usually whatever advertising money, PR personnel, direct-mail campaign capability, and so on a commercial publisher has available is likely to be directed toward those books that the publisher considers most likely to succeed, such as a book by a celebrity author, a book on a subject that is currently hot in the news, or a book by an author whose previous books have sold very well.

As a result, your publisher will probably *not* be sending you off on a book tour, nor will it be setting you up for bookstore signings, speaking engagements, or even radio or TV appearances. Instead, your publisher's decision to offer you a deal in the first place probably had more to do with its perception that you would be willing and able to orchestrate such things on your own.

I often quip (but not entirely jokingly) that the two most important features of any proposal to a publisher are (1) the book idea itself, and (2) what the author plans to do to promote and sell the book—and the second may be more important than the first! This is often literally true when a publisher signs a celebrity to write a book, say Donald Trump, for instance. At this point, The Donald can pretty much write about any business topic he wants; his name is a sure-fire guarantee that sales will be good to great simply because of who he is rather than what specifically he is writing about.

So consider the following promotional factors when preparing to pose a book idea. The more of them you can answer yes to, the more attractive your book idea will be to a commercial publisher. Your chances of landing a publisher go way up if most or all of these factors are already in place:

- Are you a public speaker who stands before 50 to 100 audiences every year, preferably audiences that average more than 500 attendees?

- Do you have lots of media contacts who have already interviewed you or quoted you on topics relating to your book idea, and who you can say with confidence will consider interviewing you again when your book comes out?
- Do you have client companies that are willing to purchase bulk copies of your new book?
- Do *you* have deep pockets of your own that can translate into a personal commitment to purchase 1,000 copies of your book for your use? How about 2,000 copies? 5,000 copies? 10,000 copies?

These are the kinds of author promotional and selling capabilities that will grab a publisher's attention.

Misconception 2

A publisher will make sure my book gets on the shelves of all the nation's bookstores, especially the largest ones.

With thousands upon thousands of books coming out each year and with hundreds upon hundreds of publishers out there pushing them, the best a commercial publisher can do here is try. Even the biggest publishing houses with the largest sales forces can only get the bookstore chains to agree to shelve a percentage of their new books, so you just can't be certain how well they will do with yours.

I have been in and around book publishing for over three decades now, and the most widespread author's lament that I have heard constantly throughout all that time and experience is: "I can't find my book in the bookstores." And it doesn't matter who the author's publishing house is, large or small. Though your publisher will attempt with gusto to get your book into the stores, no one can predict how successful that effort will be.

As with Misconception 1, publishers badly need their authors' help here. In fact, by understanding the truth about Misconception 1, that is, by personally promoting their books and making them well known, authors can provide this help. If a bookstore's customers keep coming in and asking for a certain book, that store will be sure to stock it.

Misconception 3

A publisher will endorse, print, and communicate my ideas the way I conceive them and arrange them.

Maybe, but you have to keep in mind that if a publisher is willing to invest in you, it is also going to want to have some say not only in how the book will look physically (title, cover design, interior format, size, number of pages, hardcover vs. softcover, price), but also in what it's actually going to say. This shouldn't worry you too much, as most publishers do understand that *you* are the expert here, and thus will be amenable to your leading the way contentwise. But they will assign an editor to your project whose job it will be to review your content as well as your writing style, making suggestions even for content changes all along the way.

You need to view a commercial publisher as a business partner rather than as your personal printer. Expect to make book content decisions jointly, even though this can sometimes lead to a publisher's insistence that something that you value highly be taken out or radically redone. When you accept a publisher's offer to publish your book, you are no longer going it alone. Your final product could end up looking very different from the way you originally conceived of it.

Misconception 4

A publisher will provide me with a sizable monetary advance, allowing me to take time off from my regular work so that I can focus exclusively on the book.

Now let's go back to Misconception 1. The facts about the limited resources a publisher will have for promoting your book are equally true for any pot of gold you might wish for in the form of a monetary advance. We've all read about the three million bucks Jay Leno got for his autobiography or the eight million someone gave Bill Clinton—and the *eleven* million Hillary got a year later! After all that largess, there's not much left over for the 95 percent of authors remaining on a publisher's book list.

Besides, commercial publishers have got you pegged. They realize that as a first-time author, you will accept little or no advance in return for the opportunity to be published. They also recognize that your motivation to be published has nothing to do with a desire to change your career and become a full-time book writer; instead, your book represents a marvelous marketing tool for expanding the visibility of your career or business. Since the vast majority of books published each year fail to make a profit, publishers must find ways to minimize their risks as much as possible. One obvious strategy is to keep their advance to you under, say, $5,000 (most are typically much less). They'd prefer to keep financial support of your lifestyle, as you work on your book, *out* of the equation.

Misconception 5

A publisher will keep my book in circulation long enough for it to find its audience and build a following.

Calvin Trillin, a popular *New Yorker* writer who has written many bestselling books over the last few decades, once described the typical shelf life of a book as "somewhere between milk and yogurt." Trillin made this comment to Johnny Carson on the *Tonight* show back in the 1970s, but, if anything, book shelf lives have shrunk even tighter in the years since.

Like movies and TV programs, books don't last long if they don't start selling right away. Within the first few months, your book's sales had better show some progress or your publisher will start making plans while the presses are still cooling to condemn it to "remainders." This means that your book is already on its last legs. The only place you and the public will be seeing it soon is in a bargain bin priced at just a buck or two, the publisher's not-so-subtle way of saying, "Good riddance!"

So you'd better get hopping and promote and sell your own book *but fast!* After a brief honeymoon of a month or so, your publisher will want to see some results. If it doesn't, it'll start directing its attention to other books, and yours will soon be history.

Misconception 6

A publisher will keep the book updated by coming out with revised editions.

Well, for the reasons cited in Misconceptions 1 and 4, commercial publishers are loath to invest further funds in a book, even when they should. Even when a paradigm-shifting event takes place, such as September 11 or the Berlin Wall crashing down, or when a trend that is just as momentous sets in (the rise of e-mail, online shopping, or iPods), your publisher will still resist spending any money to revise or update your book for as long as possible. This typically means a year or two, maybe even three.

Instead, your publisher might prefer that you keep promoting your book as is, wringing out every possible last nickel from the current edition, until a revised edition can be put off no longer. You can't really blame the publisher for this. Profit is an elusive prize for commercial book publishers, and yet they are indeed dependent on making a profit (why do you think they are called "commercial" publishers?), so keeping their costs down figures high on the list of tactics for winning their bottom-line wars.

Beyond these misconceptions, all of them negative realities for authors, if your goal is to use your book as a tool to leverage your business, there are two other options for you to consider. But before we review these options, let's look further at the question of what you want your book to accomplish. Your answer will dictate which option is the right one for you.

When business leaders and entrepreneurs sense the need for a book, they typically do so for a couple of reasons. The first is credibility: they feel that the time has come for them to be seen as a true thoughtleader, rightly perceiving that a book will get them there.

Second, in marketing their business, a book will serve them well as a business development tool, increasing their visibility and attracting prospects that they wouldn't otherwise know were out there.

These are certainly great reasons for wanting to publish a book. But what's often misunderstood is how those goals can clash with the very different goals of a book publisher. If an author wants to use his or her book primarily to drive up sales and increase business, a publisher has only a passing interest in having that happen. While your publisher will want you to be happy with the business development value you can extract from your book, its own self-interest has to lie in something else: selling a lot of books. If this, in turn, helps you in your business development efforts, that's fine. But if your business suffers because you had to take time off to get out and promote and sell books, the end result of that process in terms of selling books is what your publisher really needs to care about.

Again, you can't blame publishers for this, as it's a simple requisite of their own bottom line. In fact, you as an author may even have been selected because of a perception that you and/or your book concept would result in the selling of loads and loads of books. (Recall Misconception 1 here.) So as a new author, you need to be OK with making a commitment to basically taking a three-month working sabbatical so that you can spend nearly all your time just trying to sell books.

If this is *not* OK—if you've reservations about doing this because you'd rather not spend the time or the energy—two other options, both involving self-publishing, will probably make far more sense.

Now before you go running off as I drop a bomb with the words *self-publishing*, please listen up. Self-publishing today is a very different animal from what it used to be, and thus a far different animal from what you probably assume it to be. Although there are plenty of valid reasons for recoiling from the suggestion that you self-publish, your gut reaction is probably based on a very uninformed gut. In other words, things have changed.

Self-Publishing Options

Why choose self-publishing? There are two main reasons.

Motivation 1

You do not want to spend lots of time promoting and selling your book.

You see your book principally as a calling card, as a marketing device, as an indirect but most impressive "advertisement," and as a selling tool. This is typically the motivation of consultants, attorneys, and other types of professional services providers.

Motivation 2

You principally want your book as an add-on income stream for your speaking engagements.

In this case, self-publishing allows you to literally own the "product," and therefore you can make far more profit per book (per unit, that is, as your book is now a commodity) than if you were earning only a standard royalty from a commercial publisher. This is typically the motivation of those who wish to make paid speaking engagements the centerpiece of their business.

Note: At the risk of complicating things, let me add that if you are indeed a successful professional speaker who wows many, many large audiences every year, publishers may actually line up to contract you for a book. Again, refer to Misconception 1 as well as my story about the fabulous speaker I encountered in Atlanta. So, as an in-demand professional speaker, you truly could go both ways, publishing some of your books with a commercial publisher and others (in order to increase your profits) via a self-publishing method. Many of the best-known motivational speakers, such as Zig Ziglar and Larry Winget, for example, actually do things this way.

Traditionally, self-publishing has combined a high cost to the self-publishing author (for design, editing, printing, and other major expenses) with the near-impossibility of getting your self-published book reviewed and distributed for sale in bookstores. Costs alone could run from $20,000 up to the sky, depending on the author's tastes, vision, and ambition for the book. Add to this all the scurrying around that the self-published author must do to attend to a million organizational details, such as filing for copyright and an ISBN number with the Library of Congress and setting up a "fulfillment service" so that orders can be phoned in by a book buyer and shipping and handling can be arranged, and so forth.

Although fraught with headaches, this DIY (do-it-yourself) method may nonetheless be the right option for a professional speaker who wants to maintain each book as a commodity. The investment of both time and money becomes precisely that: an investment that is intended to yield an income stream perhaps 10 times greater in the first year alone, with the possibility of continuing high returns year after year after year.

One missing piece of this DIY method, however, is distribution. It can sometimes be hard to get a self-published book accepted by a major book distributor. This means that bookstores will not be able to order your book. However, nowadays we have Amazon.com, which *will* list your book, meaning that it will achieve major visibility and major accessibility online, as well as being available at your own Web site bookstore and, of course, for sale in the back of the room when you are out and about doing speaking engagements. So thanks to the Internet, distribution is no longer the bugaboo it once was.

But what about those who seek to use a published book purely as a business development tool? High profit per unit is not the prime motivation in this case, nor are these authors willing to spend all their waking hours hawking the book. It used to be that the DIY method was the only option available to such authors too, but as I said earlier, things have changed. Now we have a radically new option called POD, or print on demand. Because of the way POD companies have set themselves up, the value of this option goes far beyond the implications of print-on-demand technology all by itself. The new POD companies have also erased many of the traditional weaknesses of the DIY method.

For example, because of this paradigm-busting technology, only one copy of a book needs to be printed at a time. This means that no longer must there be an initial print run of, say, 5,000 copies at once in order to make printing the book cost-effective for the author and profitable for the printer. Books can now be printed only when they are ordered or sold, meaning that if 100 books are ordered, 100 books can be quickly printed at a profit. The costs of the POD publisher, therefore, are rock-bottom compared to those of the typical printer, translating into a one-time printing bill to the self-publishing author of only a few hundred dollars rather than the $20,000 or more required by the DIY method.

What's more, the setup of POD firms is such that they function more like a typical commercial publisher than like a printing press. A POD publisher will perform these tasks that the author must take care of under the DIY method:

- Design the book cover in conjunction with the author.
- Design the interior page format in conjunction with the author.
- Register copyright in the author's name.
- Obtain an ISBN number.
- Place the book on Amazon.com as well as with (in some cases) literally hundreds of other online booksellers.
- Sell the book on its own Web site.
- Print the book as needed and ship it out to book buyers.
- Provide a royalty to the author for each book sold, generally at a somewhat higher rate than would be given by a commercial publisher.
- Provide an author's discount of 40 percent or more.
- Arrange for the book to be available for distribution to bookstores.

This last bullet point may be the most revolutionary of all. While the age-old DIY method always meant that there was no possibility of a bookstore's ordering your self-published book, the new POD firms have eliminated this drawback through the relationships they have established with Baker & Taylor and other major book distribution companies. Although this does not mean that a POD firm will have a sales force pushing to get your self-published book on the shelves, it does mean that if someone hears about your book and walks into a local bookstore to look for it, the bookstore clerk can find it listed in a distribution catalog and respond with a pleasant, "No, we don't have it in stock, but we can order it for you!"

The POD method is obviously a huge step forward for those authors who would like to retain full control of the way their books look and read. It is kind of like hiring a commercial publisher to perform all the functions necessary to take a finished manuscript through design and production and into distribution, probably the most aggravating aspects of self-publishing.

However, if this self-publishing "heaven" sounds too good to be true, do understand that it does have drawbacks. Editing, proofreading, and indexing, for example, are not included, although some publishers may offer these services as add-ons. So POD authors must hire their own editorial professionals to ensure that their book reads clearly, is free of grammatical errors and typos, and (if they choose) contains a competent index. It is akin to walking into a copy shop with a résumé or flyer or some other "finished" document and asking for 1,000 copies. You need to make sure that your document is truly finished because the Kinko's clerk is not going to proofread it for you or offer you an editorial review. What you bring in is what you'll carry out, and the same is true for your self-published book, no matter what the method. So be sure that you and an editorial hired gun have carefully reviewed your manuscript before you contract with a POD publisher or a DIY printer to start up the presses.

The Credibility Factor

Given the realities behind the six misconceptions about getting your book published the old-fashioned way, when these are compared against the benefits of self-publishing, whether via the DIY or the POD method, what good reason for choosing the old-fashioned commercial route might still exist?

One reason might be that a good commercial publisher can help your book get better distribution through its connections with various channels such as large bookstore chains, libraries, professional associations, book-of-the-month clubs, media, book reviewers, translators, and publishers in other countries. Also, publishers are committed to, and expert in, licensing their books in ways that make both the publisher and the author more money: audio and DVD versions, electronic and digital versions, reprint editions, and even options for (if applicable) a motion picture, stage play, TV show, video game, or theme park attraction.

There's a second equally powerful issue too, one that looms over the decision to seek a publisher or go the self-publishing route like the proverbial unmentioned elephant in the room: the credibility factor.

One element that has long affected this issue is the sordid reputation and history of the "vanity presses," which are basically unscrupulous self-publishing companies that have preyed on naïve would-be authors for decades. Swooping down upon these innocent unfortunates, the typical vanity press "guarantees" publication for a flat fee of $10,000, $20,000, or $30,000, then rips a hole in its author wannabees' hearts by saddling them with cartons of badly produced, unattractive books with dashed-off cover designs, flimsy bindings, typos in the text, and little or no editing, despite promises to the contrary. The books must now be distributed somehow, but because of their pathetic look and feel, bookstores don't want to take them and reviewers don't want to review them. After a while, even showing a copy to one's friends becomes a source of embarrassment for the author. The books end up getting left in their cartons and banished to the discouraged author's basement or storage room.

Yet this scenario need never play itself out again as long as self-publishing authors (1) invest in a good professional designer and/or a self-publishing coach for help in navigating the process and instilling high quality, or (2) rely on one of the new POD firms, as most of these have dedicated themselves to creating a satisfied, loyal repeat customer base whose books boast attractive cover designs, sturdy bindings, and legible interior formats. The key is for the self-publishing author to research what's out there before making a decision to go forward. Thanks to the resources of the Internet, no one need be cheated by a vanity press ever again.

As for the issue of the *value* of the credibility provided by having your book published by a commercial publisher, think of it this way: what's primary is the "kick" from being able to quickly respond that McGraw-Hill or some other big-name publishing house, or even a little-known press, has published your book. There is certainly some value in that, just as there is in being able to boast (even in a low-key way) that you live in a particular neighborhood, belong to an excusive country club, or possess a master's degree or Ph.D. No doubt you can use this imprimatur to boost your standing with a client or prospective client or while being introduced as a program's next speaker. No doubt such a credit contributes to your expert's edge.

But if you are not able to secure a contract with a commercial publisher (whether known or unknown), or if you have decided that this is not the right choice for you, do understand the following:

- Books that are published by relatively unknown publishing houses or are self-published *can get reviewed* by book reviewers, although probably not by the *New York Times* or the *Wall Street Journal*.
- Authors of books that are published by relatively unknown publishing houses or are self-published *can secure interviews* from reporters and feature writers, although probably not by the *New York Times* or the *Wall Street Journal*.
- Authors of books that are published by relatively unknown publishing houses or are self-published *can get booked* on radio and TV programs, although probably not on the *Today* show, Larry King, or Oprah.
- Authors of books that are published by relatively unknown publishing houses or are self-published *can win speaking engagements*, although probably not as keynote speakers for the largest national conventions.

Also, realize that most people will not even ask who has published your book upon learning that you have one. Instead, most people will recognize that they themselves will never even start writing a book in their lifetime, let alone finish writing one and then actually see it come to fruition in published form. They will thus typically be very excited and impressed to learn that you have done so, and this includes many otherwise extremely accomplished professionals. Though they may idly ask, "Who published it?" your answer, whatever it is, will satisfy them. "McGraw-Hill" or a similar high-level publisher will impress them most; "Lowland Press," even though they have never heard of it, will impress them as well (it's a publisher, isn't it?); and "I self-published it" will lead to questions about the self-publishing process, which, like much of the content in this chapter, will be eye-opening and tend to make a lot of sense. What's most important for attaining your expert's edge will be the simple fact of your writing and publishing a book at all. The rest is just details.

THOUGHT NOTES

What about E-books?

The jury seems to still be out on e-books, although a few individuals have started reading such books and loving the new paradigm. However, since 95 percent of us still don't read books this way, it just doesn't seem worth the effort.

As a business development and branding tool, the impact of a book that you can hold in your hands remains immeasurable. There it is, in all its hardcover or softcover glory. Look at all those pages, look at that sparkling dust jacket—feel it in your hands! You can hand it to people and they can experience the thrill of holding it in *their* hands too and flipping through its pages. Typically they'll take a deep breath and look at you and say, "Wow! *You* did this? Marvelous! What an achievement!" Secretly they'll be wishing that they could do the same, although many of them will realize instinctively that they never will. Such reactions by others place you on a very high pedestal in their minds.

Or conversely, if they *have* published a book or two, they'll personally understand all the hard work you had to put in to make your book happen (they've been there!), raising your esteem and intellectual competence in their eyes.

In the face of all this, I just can't see how an e-book, which is so hard to grasp both visually and actually, can compete. That's not to say that things might not be changing. Those who have published e-books and make them available for purchase on their Web sites tell me they represent a steady additional revenue stream. So somebody out there seems to be reading them.

But for a major impact, my vote still goes to the old standby, a book you can hold in your hands.

If You Choose Commercial Publishing

If a commercial publisher makes the most sense for you, it's time to compose your book proposal. Many aspiring new authors mistakenly believe that the first step is to write their book. In the case of self-publishing, this is correct, but if your decision is to look for a publisher, a book proposal comes first, not a finished manuscript. Once this is completed, your next decision is to decide whether to submit your new proposal to a literary agent or directly to publishers.

The advantage of an agent, of course, is that you will have a partner and advisor who can coach you on making your proposal more effective as well as get it in front of publishers' eyes more easily. This is probably the best course for a new author, because otherwise a steep learning curve lies ahead of you, embedded with many opportunities for unnecessary mistakes. Why take the chance of blowing your initial project? Instead, pick up a published directory of literary agents or locate one on the Web and start contacting agents, asking if they would be interested in representing your idea. Contact enough of them and the chances are good that you will find one.

Before you look, however, let's get back to working on your proposal. This will help an agent evaluate your book concept and your ability to write. The standard book proposal format has six sections: "book hook," "author promotion and target market," "author bio," "competing book titles," your book's "table of contents/chapter summaries," and one or two "sample chapters." Let's look at each section in detail.

Section 1: Book Hook

Your book concept itself is what will initially grab a publisher's interest. This one- to three-page synopsis explains precisely what your book will be about and also gives details on what its readers will learn and how they might use this new knowledge in their professional and/or personal lives.

To truly grab the attention of a publisher, however, the book must have a "hook," i.e., a catchy angle that evokes a clear and immediate picture of your book's uniqueness.

An example of a strong hook comes from my client thoughtleader Suzanne Bates, president of Bates Communication, whose original proposal for her book *Speak Like a CEO: Secrets of Commanding Attention and Getting Results* (McGraw-Hill) reads like this: "A TV anchor, turned consultant-to-CEOs, reveals the secrets for success before crowds and cameras." With this book hook, Suzanne instantly grabbed the attention of her proposal readers, then followed with brief descriptions of the book's contents, issues the book would address, how the author's background qualifies her to address these issues, and how this book differs from similar books out there in bookstores now.

THOUGHT NOTES

Intriguing Book Angles

- *The Third Act: Writing a Great Ending to Your Screenplay* by Drew Yanno (Continuum International Publishing Group), a book about screenplay writing that focuses exclusively on how to write screenplay endings

- *Why Dogs Wag Their Tails: Lessons Leaders Can Learn about Work, Joy and Life* by Sherri McArdle and James Ramerman (WBiz Books), which uses stories about dogs to explore leadership issues
- *The Arch and the Path: The Life of Leading Greatly* by Michael Shenkman (Sandia Heights Media), a book depicting the arduous and joyful path leaders must take if they are to guide their organizations to success
- *Parallel Peaks: Business Insights while Climbing the World's Highest Mountains* by John McQuaig (HRD Press), which uses the author's mountaineering experiences as a metaphor for business success practices
- *Her Turn: Why It's Time for Women to Lead in America* by Vicki Donlan with Helen Graves (Praeger Press), a book that takes an advocacy stance on the advantages of women being in positions of power in companies, non-profit institutions, and politics
- *Fly Fit* by Maggie Melanson (HRD Press), a fitness book aimed specifically at those traveling by plane

Section 2: Author Promotion and Target Market

In this section, you describe your book's target market and how you're going to get its attention. Who in fact will read this book? How will you let your target readers know that your book exists? How will you convince your target readers that they should buy your book?

Again using Suzanne Bates as our model, this section of her book proposal targeted not only professionals who wished to improve their public speaking techniques and media skills but aspiring leaders in business and politics as well. Without the author's input about the book's target audience, a publisher is left to guess to whom your book will appeal, and why.

Since, as we have noted, publishers seek authors who will promote their book vigorously, this section must detail *how* you will do so. What's your promotional plan to ensure your book's success?

Section 3: Author Bio

This one- to three-page biography of the author should especially highlight your qualifications as they relate to the book's content. No publisher will take a chance on a book on, say, education by anyone other than a professional educator. Or a book on sales training by an economist. Or on management by a computer programmer. You get the idea.

You should also include here any associations that you belong to, as publishers like to know that an author is well-connected. (Again, kerching! More associations, more book sales—or so your publisher hopes!) Articles and previous books published belong here too. This speaks not only to an author's writing ability but to his or her commitment and follow-through as well.

Do you have any experience in public speaking, including a list of past (or future if you have them) speaking events? Plug those in here as well, and in Section 2 too.

Finally, the author's employment or client list should be included, as well as specific praise from relevant parties for the author's professional expertise and business results.

Section 4: Competing Book Titles

What competition will this book face? Publishers typically worry about books that face too much competition ("The market for this type of book looks glutted!") or that have been shown to sell poorly ("We tried this kind of book three years ago, and it didn't sell."). Thus, this section should explain why your book is different from the others that are out there, i.e., why readers will flock to this book as opposed to all the others.

Suzanne Bates's book, for example, was not just another book about how to improve presentation and speaking skills. There were many of those on the market when Suzanne proposed her book. In contrast, Suzanne made the case that none of the other books had targeted upper-level executives or included media skill building. How does one adequately handle interviews with newspaper and TV reporters? Not only would Suzanne's book tackle this aspect of communication, but she, the author (unlike the authors of the other books), had spent years as a TV reporter, anchor, and talk show host. Her book could offer an inside perspective for her readers that the competition could not match.

Note: Display the competition by listing five to ten competing books in this section, giving a synopsis of each one, then showing how your book will be different and, as a result, better.

Section 5: Table of Contents/Chapter Summaries

Publishers need to envision how your book will look and feel to its actual readers. So this section lists your book's table of contents, with catchy chapter titles followed by one-paragraph chapter summaries, possibly with bullets for chapter features.

What will each chapter actually cover? What issues will your readers learn about? What solutions will be provided? Will there be graphs or illustrations included? Your potential publisher will want a capsule overview of how your book's contents will look.

Section 6: Sample Chapter(s)

It can be helpful to provide a 10- to 20-page sample chapter or two, so that the publisher can get an idea of how your book will read. Although sample chapters may not ultimately end up in the book itself, they can potentially seal the deal if the publisher feels that your writing is strong and/or that the book's contents will significantly inform and "grab" its readers.

Take the time to let a few friends or colleagues read through your sample chapters; take their feedback seriously, and try to incorporate any feedback that makes sense to you. Don't automatically incorporate all the feedback you receive, however. People will always offer some kind of feedback if you request it, and some of this feedback may contradict the feedback you received from others. So don't drive yourself crazy by assuming that all the feedback you get is valid. You be the judge. You are, after all, the author, so you need to retain the final word.

Thought Notes

Involve Your Current Clients and Prospects in Your Publishing Projects

Writing a book is an excellent way to learn more about a subject, more than you might learn even by *reading* a book, as well as creating relationships with those expert thoughtleaders that you get to know during your research. In fact, your own clients, influencers, colleagues, and even prospects may fit the bill, so why not interview them as well for your book? Since most people (by far) will go through life without ever being mentioned in a book, think what a kick it would be for those business connections that end up in yours. At the very least, many of them will put this monument to *your* thoughtleading on their office bookshelves, yanking it out from time to time to show to a visitor and point out their own name in *your* book. So get them in there!

If You Choose to Self-Publish

Unlike the option of seeking a commercial publisher, self-publishing does not require creating a book proposal because self-publishing does not require anyone else's approval.

So what's the first step when you decide to go this route? That's right: begin writing!

And you don't need to contract with a printer (DIY) or a POD company first. You also don't need to hire an editor, unless you believe that an editor would be helpful to you in getting started by brainstorming with you such issues as the focus of your book, ideas for chapters, or other potential content that you may not have considered.

But even so, effectively, the first step with this option is to start writing. Once you are done, or as you complete your chapters, you can submit your draft to your hired editor, and after your work feels about done, you can start researching and choosing a printer or POD firm.

Choosing to self-publish basically means that you open the writing floodgates and let your ideas flow!

How to Actually *Write* a Book

Are there helpful hints for this stage of the process, the actual writing part? Not too many, actually. Given that a book is a lengthy project, your writing is bound to head off in a few unexpected directions, some of which could result in an even better book than the one you had originally conceived. Allow such mysterious literary meanderings to take place. But if your work strays too far afield, step back and take a careful look. If it's started to change into something very different from what your publisher expects, you risk your book's being canceled. The publisher obviously made its initial decision based on the particular concept that you presented in your formal proposal. Stray too far and the publisher may not want your radically "improved" book idea.

Is there a style or a "voice" that you should choose or emulate? Many new writers struggle with this one, fearful that if they cannot answer such a question beforehand, their writing will not have a strong enough impact. My feeling, however, is that the best way to develop your style or voice is not to try to artificially create or replicate one, but to simply write, write, write. Once you've reviewed and worked through your editor's suggestions, your natural writing voice will have emerged.

Try writing naturally, too, just like you talk. Not worrying about your style will also help you "dump" your ideas onto the screen or paper, preventing you from second-guessing yourself and feeding writer's block. It's all in your head, or most of it is, so the trick is to first get it out, in however inarticulate or awkward a form. The free flow of such an approach will bring your manuscript to life, stamping it with your personal style and voice. Refining your first draft with a second and a third will iron out all the kinks. Before long, your worries about voice, style, and other writing anxieties will recede and die as your confidence builds and your thoughtleading ideas take shape on the pages of each succeeding book.

8

Pillar 1B: Publishing Articles

This is my answer to the gap between ideas and action . . .
I will write it out!

HORTENSE CALISHER

IF PUBLISHING A BOOK gets you to the summit of Thoughtleading Mountain, publishing articles on an ongoing basis gets you at least halfway to the top. In fact, if you're not quite ready to tackle the massive commitment of writing a book, publishing articles will teach you the ropes, build your self-confidence, circulate your name and your company's name, and possibly even whet your appetite for the much higher level of thoughtleading visibility provided by a book.

Plus you'll be getting your ideas published! You've got to start somewhere.

Years ago, when I started running, I could last only a mile or two at first, but I gradually found myself working up to three miles and then to four and to five, without any feeling of strenuous extra effort. Each day I set out to run, I had built my endurance a little bit higher, so that one afternoon I found myself sailing into a fifth mile and realizing that I could, if I wanted to, keep going farther. At that moment, the thought flashed through my mind that maybe I might try running the next year's Boston Marathon.

This thought flash returned each succeeding day and grew into a hardened commitment over the next few weeks. I soon launched into a personal training schedule in which I started running in 5- and 10-K races, then in a half-marathon, then pushing myself through a few 15-mile and 18-mile training sessions.

On Patriots Day in Massachusetts, April 19, I excitedly made my way to the starting line in Hopkinton, Massachusetts, where thousands of other hopefuls awaited the noontime starting gun. With so many competing runners, it took a full five minutes for my place in the throng to reach the starting line, but from there, at 12:05, I took off down the 26.6 mile course, running, trotting, huffing, walking, and staggering my way to the finish line in Boston four hours and fifteen minutes later. I came in a full two hours after the winners, but nonetheless I had run and I had finished the grueling stretch. My achievement was substantially similar to the process that many thoughtleaders follow in order to grow their ability, self-confidence, and commitment from a mindset of writing an occasional short article to a lifestyle of continually working on one article after another, and then to writing their first full-fledged book, followed by many more books.

But even if you are already writing and publishing books, articles should still be an integral part of your repertoire. For one thing, they allow even book writers to develop new ideas; these may end up in a future book, or perhaps for one reason or another they will remain isolated, limited concepts that are not relevant to the author's next book project. But another major reason for book authors to continue to write articles is the opportunity that articles present to promote both their book and themselves. When articles are carved out of a book's chapters, these published articles can expand the book's visibility by including references to the book in the article author's bio, for example, "Ken

Lizotte is Chief Imaginative Officer (CIO) of emerson consulting group inc. in Concord, Massachusetts, which transforms business experts into thoughtleaders. This article is based on Ken's new book *The Expert's Edge: Become the Go-To Authority People Turn to Every Time* (McGraw-Hill, 2008)."

THOUGHT NOTES

Who Owns the Copyright?

You own the copyright to your article before, during, and after your article is published, explains Doug Wolf, copyright and trademark attorney-thoughtleader with Wolf Greenfield, a leading IP law firm in Boston. "In fact, you don't even have to register your article with any government agency," he explains, "because by law it is copyrighted the moment you put your words to paper or computer screen. By agreeing to let a publication print your words first, you are giving them temporary license to do so (unless you sign a contract that states otherwise), but once your article is published, you are free to republish it elsewhere if you want to and you don't even have to ask the first publication's permission to do so. All rights to your article revert back to you, automatically." Doug adds that in fact, "The only reason to wait for it to be published (in the absence of an explicit agreement to wait) is out of courtesy. Copyright law otherwise does not prevent you from publishing with others even before the original deal." He further adds, "As part of being courteous and to avoid any confusion, it is often helpful to make it clear that you are only letting them publish the article for the particular use or publication. Even though the law favors the author, it is always better to be clear with the publisher as to what permission you are granting."

What about White Papers?

When discussing articles for publications, this question frequently arises: "What about white papers?" White papers (essentially unpublished articles or case studies drawn up by an individual or company for the purpose of promoting skill sets, successful customer projects, and/or value propositions) are an age-old business tradition. Countless Web sites and résumés tout them as examples of a company's or an individual's thoughtleading prowess, as well as the indirect advertising and credibility building they provide.

But white papers have always struck me as a waste because by definition none of them are published. Someone once said to me, "Oh, you feel they're a waste because white papers are articles that can't get published."

Nope, not right. They're a waste, I replied, because they are articles that *could* have been published but never were because the author(s) never tried. Why, I always wonder, didn't they bother to go the next step?

Of course, I do know the reasons why. The author either didn't want to take the time and trouble to do so or, more likely, wasn't sure how to go about it. There may even have been some low-confidence issues going on, such as the author presuming that the white paper would not be "good enough" to get published. As a result, the opportunity to obtain bona fide third-party credibility for all the hard work and smart ideas that may have gone into this unpublished white paper was never pursued.

The Article-Publishing Process

So let's keep this from happening to *you*. To attain the expert's edge, forget white papers and go straight to published articles. You'll automatically elevate your expert status with this one continuing goal.

As is true of publishing a book, the most effective way to get articles published is not necessarily to write them first. Though it's possible to succeed this way, and some thoughtleaders do, I have found that this approach frequently frustrates would-be article authors resulting from a downward-spiral scenario: they write their article, send it off to one or two publications, then wait with bated breath to hear of its acceptance or rejection—but they hear nothing. Because they hear nothing, they assume that their writing has been deemed "bad" and decide that no one wants to publish them. But they know that they can publish their articles on their own Web sites as white papers without any waiting or anxiety, so why bother trying to get them published? Who needs the aggravation of rejection?

Unfortunately, an article submitted this way was most likely not judged to be "bad." Instead, such an unsolicited article draft may have been dismissed for other, much more mundane reasons:

- Although the article is well written, it's far too long; the author clearly did not bother to note the typical length of the articles this publication tends to run.
- Although the article is well written, its subject matter was covered thoroughly in an issue only two or three months ago; the author clearly has not reviewed the publication's most recent issues to ascertain if this topic has already been written about.
- Although the article is well written, its style is not suited to the publication's format; perhaps the article's style is academic, loaded with footnotes, whereas the publication tends to run articles that are breezier in tone, embedding notes and references into the text of the article.
- Although the article is well written, it was sent to the wrong editor, perhaps even an editor who no longer works there; the author did not confirm whom exactly such an article should be sent to.
- Although the article is well written, it was sent via snail mail, whereas this publication prefers e-mail submissions, since electronic versions of articles are easier to edit.

- Although the article is well written, the publication is entirely staff written; it *never* publishes articles written by "outsiders."

Do you get the idea? Notice that in all cases, I started with "Although the article is well written." Publication editors tend to be extremely busy beavers with high-pressure workload demands, meaning that anything out of the ordinary can throw them off the track. They simply cannot take the time to coach a new author through the basics of their publishing process. For that reason, most publications post a "writer's guidelines" section on their Web site spelling out the process for submitting an article for publication. However, many such writer's guidelines do *not* recommend querying an editor beforehand, assuming instead that your article is finished and ready to submit.

So instead of just blindly leaping off and writing your article, begin the process with a few fundamentals. First, compose a list of potential article topics, known in my vernacular as an Article Ideas List, or AIL. As the name suggests, this will be your list of all article ideas to work with, each idea being strategically aligned with your value proposition. We don't want you writing and publishing any old articles; we want your articles to express thoughtleading concepts that you will become known for, buffing up your branding and your reputation as a go-to authority that people turn to every time.

One client of mine, for example, a manufacturer of data storage systems, wanted its insurance firm customers and prospects (a favorite target market of this firm) to see how easy it was to use its recently improved data storage system. So its VP of sales wrote an article called "Storage Must Be Flexible," which was ultimately published in a major insurance trade journal.

Those who read the article learned exactly where the author was coming from in terms of knowledge and expertise, as well as the data storage company's value proposition. While an article shouldn't blatantly promote a product or service (you need to purchase an advertisement to do that!), the article nonetheless fully explored the contrasting features of competing data storage approaches, emphasizing the advantages of the type of system the author's company was in business to sell.

By beginning your article-publishing efforts with an AIL, you pitch ideas first, not entire articles, allowing editors to buy into your proposed subject matter. If your topic matches their needs, they will respond to your query with a definite go-ahead, or GO, that gives you their precise requirements, such as word count, deadline, and tone. By proceeding in this way, you save yourself from the frustration of toiling away on an in-depth article that, although it may be well written, may nonetheless end up without a home.

Creating Your AIL

In thinking through your AIL, consider many angles from which a thoughtleading topic could be approached. By creating various angles on the same basic topic, you will come up with more than one article idea (and these may be appropriate for more than one magazine). For example, if you are in sales, you might come up with two angles that are flip sides of the same coin, such as "10 Steps to Sales Success" and "The 10 Biggest Mistakes Sales Reps Make When Selling."

Other angles may be less global in scope—essentially slices of the larger topic pie. For effective selling, this might result in "How to Close a Sale," "The Importance of Qualifying Your Prospects," and "Preparing for the Sales Call." You can see that even for a fairly common topic like selling, experts can find a way to analyze their overall process, breaking it down into those components that make up the whole. In this way, the selling expert's knowledge of how to do selling well can be communicated in a variety of different ways.

In terms of pitching your ideas to editors, this strategy permits you to offer more than one option. Editors then get to pick and choose the angle they like, increasing the odds that one of your ideas will be picked, rather than receiving a pitch that's a take-it-or-leave-it proposition.

In terms of how much information on your topic an editor needs, many writers (experienced as well as neophytes) and PR representatives shove far too much information the poor editor's way, including lengthy, detailed article outlines, a cover letter, a full author CV, even a PDF or snail-mailed marketing/press kit. Yet the truth is that all an editor really cares about is the nub of the idea.

So my recommendation is that you e-mail two to four ideas from your AIL (so as not to overload the editor), formatting each idea as a one-paragraph headline and "blurb." You might also include a one-line bio, but more than that can be too much, since the editor will assume that you must be a qualified expert in this area if you care enough to write an article about it. Just give editors the basic information that they need in order to make their decision about giving you a GO. Any follow-up communication from there can expand upon your initial information.

What will your e-mail pitch look like once you've got your AIL in place and you're ready to roll? Here's an example from our fictional selling thoughtleader (we'll call him Steven Expertise) to Jim Journal, the editor of *Selling Prowess* magazine (both also fictional):

Hello Jim,

Below are a few article ideas I believe your readers would find useful. Let me know if you would like me to work on one or more of them for you. I am a veteran professional sales consultant with clients in 45 states:

"10 Steps to Sales Success"
This article covers 10 points that can spell the difference between selling success and selling failure. Real-life examples of each point can be included in the text. Graph also available.

"10 Biggest Mistakes When Selling"
Selling professionals often fail to realize when they are making a fatal mistake that is sure to send their prospect running for cover. This article describes 10 of the most common (and

disastrous) selling mistakes and how sales reps can correct such behavior to ensure that they never make such mistakes again.

"How to Close a Sale"

Closing a sale can be hard or simple. Unfortunately, without observing the age-old fundamentals of effective selling, many reps make this final stage of the selling process both very hard and repeatedly unsuccessful. This article explains how closing a sale can be achieved in a manner that maximizes the result for both the sales rep and the new customer. An illustrative table of poor closing techniques can be included.

    P.S.: Here's a link to my Web site: www.salescu.com. Thanks in advance for your attention!

Regards,

Steve Expertise, Director
Sales Consultants Unlimited

And that's it! Simple, right? But what more does Jim Journal need to know? Now he can choose one or more of these topics, then e-mail back his GO. Typically, here's how such a response will look:

Thanks, Steve, for these ideas. Yes, your third idea would be perfect for our December issue, as we have not written too much about closing techniques. I am sure our readers would love to hear some good pointers.

    Can you send me a 1,000-word article by November 1? Please include your bio and a head and shoulders e-photo as well.

Thanks for your interest in writing for our publication!

Best,

Jim Journal, Editor
Selling Prowess magazine

There now. Isn't that a tad more pleasant than snail-mailing your long-winded 3,000-word article about every aspect of selling to a half-dozen publications and then hearing nothing from any of them for your trouble? With this method, even before you've submitted your article, you've already gotten a commitment from a genuinely interested editor. Assuming that you do even the most basic job of putting together your article, your new editor will keep his promise of including you in his December issue. The rest, as they say, will soon be publishing history!

THOUGHT NOTES

No Moolah

Are you wondering why I haven't mentioned how much compensation you might earn directly from a publication that you have granted the privilege of publishing your masterpiece? Sorry, there's not much to say here. Except in rare instances, publications simply do not budget any money at all for paying their expert authors. Any budget they do have for compensation is saved for their freelance writers, i.e., independent journalists who write for a living. Even for them, the pay is not great.

Publications know that since you are an expert, your motivation for writing articles is to raise your business visibility and increase your relatively lucrative business revenue. Your articles essentially represent free advertising for you, and publications know this. Therefore, they offer you space in their pages in return for your article, but that, they feel, is enough. So don't even bother to ask!

Targeting the Right Publications

Once you finish composing your AIL (5 to 10 good ideas should be enough), it's time to put together a list of your target publications. Just as you don't want to write any old article on any old topic, you also don't want to get your article published in any old publication. For the most part, for example, most mainstream newspapers are out because either they serve too few readers or their business focus is minimal. Notable exceptions are the *Wall Street Journal* and the largest metropolitan dailies, although the relatively small amount of space that these newspapers have available for outside contributions makes them also generally not worth the effort.

Instead, concentrate on dedicated business and industry publications, as these (1) will always be looking for contributions from business experts such as you, and (2) are read by highly focused target business audiences. To be sure you choose the right publications from among the thousands that exist, consider these questions:

1. *Who hires you?* This means the actual decision maker, executive level, department, function, type of company, industry, and so on that represents your target markets.
2. *Who influences those who hire you?* If there are certain professionals or managerial levels or departments in a company that typically influence the decision maker who hires you, then target journals read by them too. If they are already good at spreading the word about you, then educate

more and more of them about your valuable expertise, expanding your referral circle ever wider.

A few examples:

- Are you typically brought into a company by the CEO, the president, or the founder/owner? If so, publications with names like *CEO* magazine, *President's Forum*, or *Business Owner's Digest* might be right for you.

- Maybe HR professionals or training managers typically hire you. Put on your target publication list such titles as *HR Focus*, *HR Executive*, *Training & Development Magazine*, and *Training World*.

- Perhaps you work exclusively in a particular industry, such as for manufacturers of medical devices. You'll want to put on your list such publications as *Medical Devices Weekly*, *Medical IT Products*, *Medical Instruments* magazine, and *Med Device Manager*.

- Do CPAs tend to refer business your way? Put *CPA Journal* and *CPA Today* on your TPL (Target Publications List).

- Do attorneys send prospects your way? Pitch to *Lawyers' Weekly*, *Executive In-House Counsel*, and *National Legal Reporter*.

There are also cross-industry publications to consider. These publications address issues that appeal to readers in every industry and on many levels of the corporate organizational chart. Such publications include *Industry Week*, *US Industry Today*, *USA Business*, and their regional counterparts with names like *Boston Business Journal*, *Atlanta Business Journal*, and *Silicon Valley News*.

The idea is to align the publications you target with your business's strategic objectives. When Brad Hosmer, president of the Beta Consulting Group, a marketing consulting firm based in New Hampshire, began writing articles about how "old-line industries," e.g., manufacturing, automotive, and textiles, could gear themselves up for today's more turbulent, unpredictable times, he needed to zero in on publications read by the highest-level decision makers in those industries. "These companies were used to going on year after year without much change or challenges from their markets," he recalls. "All of a sudden, as the new century came upon them, they couldn't ignore the changes any more."

It made sense, therefore, for Brad to submit his articles to publications like *US Industry Today* and the *Handbook of Business Strategy*, many of whose readers were at the helm of such "stodgy" old-line firms. Brad's article topics also had to be drawn from his core expertise and focused on precisely the recommendations he was finding himself making to his core customers. So such article topics as "Can a Corporate Old Dog Learn New Tricks?" and "Going Global: Should You or Shouldn't You?" were pitched to editors of both industry and strategy-focused publications. Before long, GOs were flowing steadily and Brad's article credits began to pile up.

So stock your TPL with publications read by your target markets so that you maintain your focus on the types of readers you want to reach. You can find editor contact information either on a publication's Web site or in directories located in your library or bookstore. You might also ask your clients directly what they read or you might take note of the publications in their offices or reception area. Don't be afraid to ask them to borrow a copy of an unfamiliar publication or to at least get the name of its Web site. Then, armed with all this editorial treasure, get busy e-mailing your article pitches.

Do not use snail mail, by the way, no matter what you may hear or read anywhere else. E-mail makes this process frightfully simple, and your days are busy enough without introducing cumbersome, previous-century procedures. By using e-mail, you'll make life easier for both yourself and your editors. And making life easier for your editors is 90 percent of what it's all about.

Deciding What to Pitch, and to Whom

I mentioned before that you should probably pitch from two to four ideas at a time. How, then, do you decide which ones to include? One way is to search a publication's Web site for its editorial calendar, which is typically a full year's listing of editorial themes, issue by issue. Such an "ed cal" might also be found in a directory supplied by your library or one you purchased from a bookstore. This schedule can be invaluable in helping you determine just which topics the publication might be looking for. You can add this information to your pitch this way: "The first two topics might work for your 'Selling Fundamentals' special issue in January, and the last two for your 'Closing Techniques' special issue in July."

When you pitch, by the way, don't pitch to just one or two publications. Send out a minimum of 10 pitches each time: the more the merrier. This will increase your odds, and the likelihood that a publication will be bothered by your multiple pitches is slim. And don't expect many rejection e-mails. Although you may get one or two now and then, most editors will just ignore your ideas if those ideas don't work for them, feeling too busy to bother with a reply. Don't take this personally, and do not scratch these publications off your list. Sooner or later, one of your future ideas is bound to hit the mark and, when it does, you'll hear from the previously unresponsive editor, this time filled with enthusiasm.

Occasionally you'll actually receive a courteous response from an editor, thanking you for your ideas but confessing that none of them are right for her publication at the moment. She will probably add an invitation for you to keep pitching your ideas, and she may even ask if you have other ideas to pitch right here and now. When this happens, scurry over to your AIL and zip back two to four more ideas ASAP. The odds are great that this time she will respond with a request for one of these additional ideas. Then you'll truly understand why this AIL device is such a superior way to go.

THOUGHT NOTES

Article Tidbits

The most visible, first-tier publications such as *Forbes*, *Fortune*, and *BusinessWeek* do *not* take articles from outside experts, except for the occasional guest columnist. These publications employ staff writers to produce virtually all their articles. So skip past these admittedly desirable vehicles and instead seek out trade journals, professional journals, business weeklies, newsletters, online information sites, and other second-, third-, fourth-, and even fifth-tier publications. The point is to get published on a regular basis, so don't become fixated on specific media targets.

Overcoming "Writers' Fright"

After obtaining a GO from an editor to submit an article, many new writers, amazingly, fail to follow through. Perhaps they couldn't discipline themselves to block out even an hour or two to write the article, or perhaps they found themselves overwhelmed by the issue of how to put down their ideas in an article format. Such personal blocks boil down to what I call "writer's fright," i.e., the fear that one's writing efforts will ultimately be rejected, and therefore attempting to write is not worth the effort. Those who conquer writer's fright, however, often report that the hardest part of writing was just getting started. Once you are over that hurdle, the rest of the process often flows relatively easily.

If writer's fright has its hooks into *you*, keep a few points in mind to loosen its grip. First of all—pay attention, now—you don't have to be the next Hemingway or J. K. Rowling to write and publish business articles. As a knowledge expert, you merely have to know your stuff and push it out of your head. Thus, bravely sit down and dump whatever relevant concepts and words you've got in there, without worrying about how it all sounds. Once you have got it all out, you can then go back and polish up the way you've expressed it. But the main thing to do first is simply regurgitate it.

If that doesn't work, there are other steps you might take to rid yourself of this paralysis. Thinking through how your article will ultimately look could be the key to bolstering your confidence about your final product. So try the following:

1. *Decide on the core message of your article.* Make sure this writing project will be consistent with both your marketing objectives and your core values. What one message do you most want your readers to hear? Let the answer to this be your anchor as you move along through the actual writing process.

2. *Are you an "outline person" or not?* Some people (like me) work well with only the skimpiest of outlines. Others feel the need for a detailed overview of their article's points. Know which category you belong to. If you're an outline person, sketch one out, listing your main topics, main subtopics, sub-subtopics, potential examples, and supporting data. By the time you're done, you may have 50 percent or more of the article's content written out.

   If you are not an outliner, whip up a very bare-bones outline to help you see where you're going, then move on. Or don't spend any time at all on an outline! Usually the best thing a nonoutliner can do is just burst out of the starting gate.

3. *Begin, begin, begin!* To elaborate on my previous advice about just dumping out your ideas without worrying about how they read, new writers often bog themselves down by attempting to craft the perfect word or sentence right from the get-go. Sometimes they move along to the second sentence only after they have exhaustively perfected the first. The labor and intensity of this process is both wearing and time consuming. Giving up the project altogether is a logical result.

   Instead, try banging out the roughest draft imaginable as quickly as possible. Pretend you've got an overdue e-mail memo to get out and start typing furiously. Think: *I've got to get this thing out now.* Do not fret about how the thing reads or whether someone may laugh at it. Just push the information out of your head fast, fast, fast. Once you've finished, push back from your desk—and breathe.

If you do this, 90 percent of what you dump into your Word document will have poured out in a fairly logical order. What you'll now have is a first draft that you can return to and rework. You'll have defeated your writer's fright.

4. *Research, anyone?* Sometimes your article will require checking up on some facts, inserting a graph or a grid, or even conducting a few field interviews. If you do this research before you begin the actual writing, you may end up feeling confident that you have all the data you need to fill in gaps that you previously weren't sure of. This may also help you hurdle your writer's fright and get your draft going.

5. *Revise, revise, revise.* A writer friend of mine, Gary Provost, the author of over 20 books and hundreds of published articles, used to say, "I never worry about the first draft because I know I will always have time to go back over it and make whatever changes it needs." Adopt this outlook in your writing process and you'll probably cease being terrified by it.

6. *Show as well as tell.* As you revise your first and second drafts, watch for places in your article where you might throw in an example to illustrate a point. Newer writers often forget this, leaving their readers to ponder abstract descriptions that are hard to visualize. For example, an article about cell phone problems might illustrate one of its points with an anecdote about how a user reacts when a call gets dropped. My cell phone example here is in fact an example of showing as well as telling.

7. *Dispense advice.* Have you remembered to include a prescriptive section near the end of your article so that readers will have some idea of what to do with all your wisdom? It's easy to get caught up in the enthusiasm of explaining a few core article concepts, then wind up the article without offering a few tips and takeaways. But since

your credibility will be well established by this point in your article, your thoughtleading advice not only will be appreciated but is likely to be heeded as well.

8. *Ignore word count—until now.* Each article demands a different manuscript length (set, of course, by your editor), but don't worry about this at first; just write. Worrying about word count too early will bog you down as you attempt to micromanage what you have to say. It's better to go too long, then cut words and whole sections as you revise, revise, revise. That way, you'll give your concepts plenty of room to develop, tightening up the way you express them in a later draft.

If, by the way, your word count comes out too short, simply expand your points with additional explanations and/or more examples. You might even have room to add more points to your core concept, points that you may have assumed you were not going to have room for.

Feedback and Submission

Once your article is completed to the best of your ability, solicit a trusted friend or colleague or (better yet) a professional editor to review your draft and offer some feedback. Incorporate some of this feedback before submitting the article to your waiting editor. I say "some" because you don't necessarily want to automatically incorporate all the feedback you receive, since some of it might be at odds with your gut. Allow yourself to be the final arbiter of whether feedback gets incorporated or not. All you want to do is gain some perspective, because by now you have gotten way too close to your article, making it hard to know how it reads to someone else.

THOUGHT NOTES

Involve Your Clients and Prospects in Your Publishing Projects

While publication of your articles will provide a powerful vehicle for your business development efforts, don't neglect the use of the writing process itself as a business development tool. By interviewing your clients, influencers, and even prospects for your articles, you establish a relationship with them that instantly causes them to view you as a thoughtleader rather than just another vendor. They will see you as a true expert even as you are asking them their thoughts on topics on which *they* are the expert. They will also be excited to see their name in print, providing you with more positive relationship touch points.

A note of caution: always let people review the portion of the article in which you have written about them and/or have quoted them before your final submission of the article for publication. You don't want them to have any negative surprises. Let them change what you have written unless their change alters your article's accuracy and integrity. You are not, after all, writing a journalistic epic, so don't be afraid of some minor collaboration with those you interview. I don't recommend, however, that you show interviewees your entire article, unless you wish them to review it because you value their advice. Otherwise, what is in the rest of your work is none of their business.

Don't solicit too much feedback, however. If you ask for 100 critiques, you'll get 100 critiques. Many of these will contradict each other. Some will tell you to do things that you already had decided not to do, others will say that you should scrap the project altogether, and still others will wonder why you didn't include things that you know you know nothing about! With feedback, there comes a point when enough is enough. Too much feedback, despite any gains beforehand, could easily reinstate your writer's fright.

Finally, when you are ready to submit your article to your editor, submit it with humility. A helpful attitude to adopt, no matter how hard you've worked, is: "Now I'll find out what's really *wrong* with it." This way, you've prepared yourself for a potential request to revise the article drastically, answer a few editorial questions, or make additions in areas that you thought you had adequately addressed. The good news is that this rarely entails a whole lot of extra work. More likely your editor will request small changes here and there, in effect readying your article for publication. Once that process ends, you'll be scheduled for an upcoming issue, then asked by your new editor, "What can we work on next?"

9

Pillar 2: Speaking to Groups and Followers

Think like a wise man but communicate in the language of the people.

WILLIAM BUTLER YEATS

PUBLIC SPEAKING COUPLED with publishing delivers a one-two punch that your nonthoughtleading competitors simply cannot match. While your competitors blissfully hand out ho-hum copies of their Power-Point displays or glossy marketing materials to their audiences, you need only offer a reprint of your most relevant or recent published article. This reprint is sworn testimony to attendees that you are special—an expert with an edge, a genuine thoughtleader. They are lucky to be listening to you!

Smart professionals well understand the value of relationship building in developing and keeping new business. What better vehicle is there for relationship building than an event at which lots of high-level business folks will show up in one place to listen to *you*?

An added bonus is the promotion you gain by having your name, your firm's name, your bio, and your thoughtleading credentials published in the conference brochure, which is mailed out to thousands upon thousands of successful professionals.

For all these reasons, speaking is something that you must pursue. Do you value meeting people one-on-one? Speaking multiplies the benefits of such encounters by maximizing your relationship-building efforts. Choose the right topic and the right audience and you'll frequently be pleasantly surprised at how fruitful speaking can be.

For thoughtleaders, speaking provides value in other ways as well, contributing to you personally as well as professionally:

1. Preparing a presentation helps you *organize and deepen your thoughts*.
2. Speaking forces you to *think quickly on your feet*, economizing and refining the way you articulate your ideas and your value proposition.
3. Fielding audience questions helps you *perceive your own concepts in a new light*. You may be asked something that you hadn't thought about before, leading to new research on your part, or you may hear an attendee describe a personal experience that bolsters your case.
4. Speaking provokes speaker-audience sharing, *spawning new thoughts* that can be absorbed by speaker and audience alike.

But I'm Afraid to Speak!

It's an age-old maxim that when surveys are taken of the general populace, many people report that they fear public speaking more than they fear death! If that's you, let's get over this right now. But my ordering you to be brave may not be sufficient to get you there. So review these suggestions for getting you off your nervous duff and up to the front of the room:

- *Take a course or join Toastmasters.* Find a way to practice speaking in a safe setting. There are public speaking courses galore at colleges and community adult education centers. There's also Toastmasters International, an informal speaking practice club found in most regions, usually meeting in a library or local hotel. Individuals of all stripes get together to coach one another on speaking skills. You should also check out the National Speakers Association, which probably sponsors a chapter near where you live. This professional association will get you past your amateur status so that you can fully integrate public speaking into your thoughtleading repertoire.
- *Speak, speak, speak.* Find as many places to speak as you can. You'll experience ups and downs, and there will be times when you wish you had never gotten up on that stage, but if you keep at it, you'll turn out a better speaker for having done so, experience being the proverbial best teacher.
- *Recognize opportunities.* Notice how many mini-opportunities abound for speaking, many of which could be easily passed by. Sometimes seemingly mundane situations can be beneficial not only for practicing speaking but for promoting your thoughtleading brand as well.

So when a program host invites audience attendees to stand up and give their "30-second elevator speech," you should jump right up and be the first to go. Not only will you be grabbing an unexpected chance to practice, but what you say in those 30 seconds may put you as much in the spotlight as the keynote speaker.

For example, my elevator speech, which I call an "impact statement" thanks to relationship capital expert Jim Masciarelli, the thoughtleader who designed it, typically gets me great attention from an audience because it hits them squarely where they live. My impact statement follows Masciarelli's careful construction as described in his book *PowerSkills*:

"Hello, my name is Ken Lizotte, I'm with emerson consulting group," I begin, then after a momentary pause (for effect), I say, "where we *make business experts famous!*

"We do this by helping them get their ideas published, thereby positioning them as leading thinkers in their field. If you'd like to gain more recognition in your target market as an expert with an edge, see me tonight or send me an e-mail."

Then I sit down as many in the room murmur and plan to approach me later and grab my business card. It gets 'em every time!

Preparing for Speaking

One question that vexes many new speakers is what conference and meeting planners are looking for. This is actually not a naïve question because professional events typically do have themes, and speaking standards vary from event to event, so unless you review an event's speaker guidelines and past agendas carefully, you could be barking up the wrong tree in your attempt to secure a speaking spot there.

For example, many legal or engineering associations prefer to stress topics that are professional-technical in nature, such as seminars on new regulations, changes in laws, or new technological developments. If your expertise falls within such categories, you may find yourself in demand for speaking slots at such events. But if your speaking topics fall into broader categories, such as leadership skills, sales skills, or work-balance techniques, winning an invitation to speak to these associations will be improbable at best.

On the other hand, many event sponsors do seek such broader topics, even if your understanding of these areas is not industry-specific. This means that you can easily adapt your topics to a wide variety of such conference venues. For example, my speaking topic, "Becoming a Thoughtleader," has been offered to such disparate audiences as management consultants, Harvard students, foreclosure practitioners, and self-employed nutritionists.

The fundamental question to ask when you are considering topics to offer has to do with you and your expertise. It's the same question you asked when we explored how to choose topics for books and articles, that is, what do I want to be known for?

THOUGHT NOTES

Introductions

It's a good idea to bring your own introduction to your speaking engagements and hand it to whoever will be introducing you. Frequently, you'll be asked anyway how you want to be introduced, and if you respond with the equivalent of "However you like," you could end up with an introduction that doesn't quite do the job. If you're going to spend a lot of time crafting speaking topics that accentuate the thoughtleading focus you want to be known for, why leave your intro to chance?

Prepare your own introduction, then bring a copy that's nicely printed out and easy to read. Your introducer will be most grateful that you did.

Your STL

Your STL, or Speaking Topics List, will be identical, or nearly so, to your AIL (Articles Ideas List). The best speaking topics are those that are aligned with your business objectives and the reputation as an expert that you want to cultivate. Recognize that your writing and speaking should overlap to such an extent that the lines separating them blur. In other words, an article can be a chapter in your book and also a speaking topic. A chapter in a book can be a speaking topic and also an article. A speaking topic can be an article and also a book chapter. And so on.

What does this look like? Again, to compose your STL, refer to the format of your AIL. Although most major conferences will require you to fill out a formal proposal document listing your topic's "learning points" and "takeaways" and perhaps an outline of your presentation and other details, less particular situations (such as an association chapter meeting, a Rotary Club, or a civic organization) are more likely to request only your topic title and a "short description." Thus, your STL should look like this:

Speaking Topics List

Ken Lizotte

Getting Your Ideas Published
Extend your visibility and deepen your credentials with a book or article about your special expertise and knowledge. Publishing promotes you and your business, organizes your thinking, and broadens your array of services. This session will show you how to get your publishing program off the ground.

Thoughtleading: The Art of Separating
Your Business from the Competitive Pack!
What separates the winners of business from all the rest? Those who practice "thoughtleading" reach the top of their profession, earn the lion's share of business, attain the highest rungs of income . . . and stay there! In this program, Ken shows how becoming a "thoughtleader" can separate your company from your competition, elevating you to the top of your game.

The Expert's Edge: Become the Go-To
Authority People Turn to Every Time
If you're already an expert, your next step is to acquire "the expert's edge." In this session, you'll learn tools for rising above your competition and positioning yourself as the go-to authority that your target market will turn to every time. Competition will become a thing of the past.

You can see here that by changing a word here and there—replacing *article* or *book* with *program* or *session*—you can use the exact same descriptive blurb for a speaking topic on your STL that you used in your AIL. You may also imagine how your speaking topics can be customized for very different audiences without changing anything in the blurb. For example, I have used my "thoughtleading" topic in the following ways:

- "Thoughtleading: The Art of Separating Your Law Practice from the Competitive Pack!"
- "Thoughtleading: The Art of Separating Your Coaching Services from the Competitive Pack!"
- "Thoughtleading: The Art of Separating Your CPA Firm from the Competitive Pack!"
- "Thoughtleading: The Art of Separating Your Job Search Campaign from the Competitive Pack!"

Just by substituting the appropriate professional terminology, the speaking topic becomes available to a whole new audience. In this way, you keep modifying your original STL so that new professional groups view your proposed presentation as having been specially prepared for them—and no one else!

Target Audiences List (TAL)

Next comes fundamental question number two: to whom should I speak? Again, recall the principles of our article planning. Just as you needed to develop a list of target publications, here you'll create a document called a TAL, or Target Audiences List, filled with organizations whose members might hire you or influence people who might hire you. Here's the same list I provided in the chapter on publishing articles, customized for speaking:

- Are you typically brought into a company by the CEO, the resident, or the founder/owner? If so, groups with names like the CEO Club, the Young Presidents' Club, or Entrepreneurs' Network might be right for you.

- Maybe HR professionals or training managers typically hire you. Look at such groups as SHRM (Society of Human Resources Management), ASTD (American Society of Training & Development), or the Organizational Development Network.
- Perhaps you work exclusively in a particular industry, such as for manufacturers of medical devices. You'll want to list the Association for the Advancement of Medical Instrumentation and the Medical Device Manufacturers Association.
- Do CPAs tend to refer business your way? Try speaking at the annual conferences of the ASCPA (American Society of Certified Public Accountants) and the Association of American Accountants.
- Do attorneys send prospects your way? You'll want to pitch to the American Bar Association, the National Lawyers Guild, and the In-House Counsel Attorneys of America.

Finally, there are the cross-industry and cross-profession associations that gather audiences from many different industries and professions and at many levels of corporate organizations. Such groups include the U.S. Chamber of Commerce, the National Business Association, the Executive Committee, and the Conference Board.

Don't forget, too, that plenty of such organizations will be thriving right there on your home turf, including local chapters of national organizations, local chambers of commerce, independent groups with no national affiliation, and even companies that are on the lookout for lunchtime or special-events speakers.

To find a list of organizations and events, visit your library or scan the Internet. Your library will carry a directory or two with titles like *Directory of Professional & Trade Organizations* or *Directory of Annual Conferences and Meetings*. Such volumes will provide details of thousands of groups that are seeking speakers for their monthly, quarterly, and/or annual events. The information provided will include dates of events, locations, speaker guidelines, contact information, Web site URL, and so on.

If you get really serious about speaking, you might actually purchase a copy of one of these directories, so that you don't have to keep
running down to the library every time you need to do some research.
You might never make a more lucrative investment.

Speaker Sheet

To communicate your value as a speaker quickly, succinctly, and
clearly, create a "speaker sheet." This one-page document can be
posted on your Web site, e-mailed as a PDF, or handed out as a paper
document to instantly convey all relevant information pertaining to
your speaking credentials. It includes your bio, photo, topics, publishing credits (including a graphic of your most recent book cover, if any),
speaking testimonials, and contact information.

As an example, mine appears on the next page.

When you are asked for information about yourself as a speaker,
this tool makes it easy for you to respond, "Sure thing. I'll e-mail you
my speaker sheet right now." It simplifies the process of promoting
yourself as a speaker and saves everyone a lot of time.

Obtaining Gigs

When it comes to actually obtaining speaking engagements, setting up
your STL and TAL can at first glance be strikingly similar to setting
yourself up for publishing articles. However, once your tools are in
place, the similarity ends. Unlike pitching article ideas, successfully
obtaining speaking gigs involves so many variables that an entirely different plan of action must be engaged.

Consider the many directions in which your hunt for audiences
can go: Some organizations are easy to approach and are always on the
lookout for speakers of any kind (Rotary Clubs), so that merely
approaching them (by phone or e-mail) may be enough to secure a gig.
Other organizations require a formal proposal in their own format; thus,

emerson consulting group, inc.

Transforming Experts into Thoughtleaders

Ken Lizotte CMC

Long-time thoughtleader Ken Lizotte CMC is CIO (Chief Imaginative Officer) of emerson consulting group inc. (emersongroup). Over the years, Ken has been interviewed by Newsweek, Business Week, Fortune Magazine, CBS-TV, Writer's Digest, and many others. Author of The Expert's Edge: Become the Go-To Authority People Turn to Every Time (McGraw Hill, 2008) and four previous books, he is a popular keynote speaker on such topics as becoming a thoughtleader, getting books and articles published, and unlocking creativity, motivation and enthusiasm. Currently on the National Board of Directors of the Institute of Management Consultants USA, Ken holds the desirable CMC (certified management consultant) designation. He is also a seminar leader at Harvard University and co-founder of the National Writers Union.

emerson consulting group, inc.

www.thoughtleading.com
box 41, concord, ma 01742
978-371-0442
fax 413-521-0013
ken@thoughtleading.com

Speaking Titles

KEN LIZOTTE

Thoughtleading: the Art of Separating Yourself from the Pack

What separates the leaders of business competition from all the rest? Those who practice "thought leadership" reach the top and stay there. Ken shows how becoming a thought leader delivers competitive advantages second to none, and how you too can join the ranks of such winners.

Getting Your Ideas Published

Learn to extend your visibility and deepen your credentials with a book or article about your special skills and knowledge. Publishing promotes you and your consulting practice, organizes your thinking and frequently broadens your array of services.

Unlock Your Creativity and Enthusiasm!

In this program, Ken shows how drawing upon one's innate creativity, passion and enthusiasm can advance professional (and personal) objectives.

Balancing Work and Family

Frazzled? Overworked? Stressed? Drawn from material from Ken's book Balancing Work and Family, this program helps get attendees into lasting career-personal balance. Includes effective tools and advice for identifying and pursuing desired goals.

Client Services

emersongroup services are guaranteed and include one or all of the following:

• Developing and placing by-lined articles in major publications

• Arranging speaking engagements at important conferences and meetings

• Generating media interviews and free publicity

• Developing original research projects

• Guiding book projects and book promotion campaigns

"Every semester since 1989 I have presented a lecture to college students on leadership in which I define communication this way: 'To master and practice leadership's exchange, read and write, listen and speak.' You could give that part of the lecture with ease. Thanks for a fabulous presentation, Ken."

—Fred W. Green, Chairman
CEO Club of Boston

"Thanks for speaking at the Monday Network last week. Everyone loved you, and found your presentation very motivating. Frankly, I haven't seen them that inspired in a long time. Hope you'll agree to come back again some day."

—Bob Richard, Director
Monday Network

Clients:

Keane Inc. • The Levinson Institute
MIT Enterprise Forum • The Arch of Leadership
The IP law firm of Wolf Greenfield
Mitretek Healthcare • The Consulting Exchange
Longfellow Benefits Associates
Peak Financial Management
Intertech Engineering Associates

---

any boilerplate you have crafted may be useful in parts but will not necessarily be transferable as a whole. Still other organizations require a DVD of one of your past performances (although most won't), while others will tell you that they select only via committee and only at certain times during the year, such as June or December. Variations of individualized procedures such as these for selecting speakers are endless.

So how does one get a handle on all these myriad selection processes? Unfortunately, the only good way to do so is to roll up your pant cuffs and wade right in. You'll be treading water before too long and swimming through heavy swells and squalls. But eventually you'll get to the other shore as the system actually begins to make a little sense.

THOUGHT NOTES

Sponsor Your Own Presentations and Seminars

Many organizations tout the value of sponsoring their own seminars at which their in-house thoughtleaders do most or all of the presenting. Sometimes experts from other organizations are invited to share a panel; other times it's an in-depth "boot camp" in which the organization's lead expert shares everything that he or she knows. Typically the majority of attendees will be prospects, often leading to their signing on for longer engagements.

The Importance of Being an Author

One tenet we touched upon back when we explored publishing a book was the impact of a book in positioning you as a thoughtleader extraordinaire. In fact, being the author of a book is the single most important factor in getting chosen for speaking assignments, particularly at the most desirable conferences and meetings. While anyone can dream up a PowerPoint presentation, draft a white paper, or paste together original handouts, it takes a lot more time, skill, endurance, commitment, and follow-through to publish a book. Also, the credibility kick from having done so (even when a book is self-published) dwarfs all other credentials by a country mile.

That's why when meeting planners sit down to pore over their stack of speaker proposals, they stick like glue to proposals from the author of a recent book. And if an author's book is truly hot, so much the better. So get started writing and publishing your book. Though you will still be able to obtain speaking assignments without a book, especially at smaller venues and if you've been at least publishing articles, more than any other single tactic, book authorship will kick your speaking gig success rate into high gear and send it soaring.

Proposals and Inquiries

Now look at your Target Audiences List and begin at the top, proposing yourself as a speaker to each group on the list. Fill out Web site proposal forms for those groups on the list that require them. For less formal groups, prepare an e-mail for the meeting planner, association director, or program chair, attaching your speaker sheet.

In your e-mail note, be brief. If someone referred you to this group, drop that contact's name right away. Structure your e-mail note like this:

Hello Jim,

Bob MacGruff suggested that I contact you about speaking at one of your Sales Reps of America chapter events. Bob thought my experience and insights might be of value to your members and program attendees.

Below are three of my more popular speaking topics. I am a veteran professional sales consultant with clients in 45 states, and the author of a new book called *Selling Made Easy* as well as numerous articles published in such journals as *Selling Power* magazine, *Sales Weekly*, and *Sales/Marketing Management Monthly*:

"10 Steps to Sales Success"

This presentation covers 10 points that many sales reps forget but that can spell the difference between selling success and selling failure. Real-life examples of each point can be included in the presentation.

"10 Biggest Mistakes When Selling"

Selling professionals often fail to realize when they are making a fatal mistake that is sure to send their prospect running for cover. This workshop explains 10 of the most common (and disastrous) selling mistakes and adds a hands-on exercise designed to teach participants how to correct such behavior so that they will never make such mistakes again.

"How to Close a Sale"

Closing a sale can be hard or simple. Unfortunately, without observing the fundamentals of effective selling, many reps make this stage of the selling process both hard and repeatedly unsuccessful. This presentation details how closing a sale can be achieved in a manner that maximizes the result for both the sales rep and the new customer. An illustrative PowerPoint of poor closing techniques can be included.

I've also attached my speaker sheet containing my bio, additional speaking topics, testimonials, and more. If you'd honor me with an invitation to speak before your group, I'd be pleased to do so.

Thanks in advance for your attention!

Best regards,

Your Name

This sample e-mail should have a familiar ring to it, as it's essentially the same format suggested for e-mailing article pitches. The only substantive difference might be that it paints a fuller picture of the speaker himself. That's because, unlike publications, meeting planners have to worry about how personable and articulate a speaker will be. For that reason, you should give the meeting planner a chance to see a little of that along with your expertise and credentials.

But follow the rules of KISS: keep it simple, stupid. No dumping of top-heavy marketing kits and books and lengthy topic outlines. Less is always more when it comes to selling yourself. Give meeting planners a chance to take in your introduction and make the next move, which could look something like this:

Thanks, Steve, for these speaking ideas. Yes, your second idea would be perfect for our April networking event, as we have all made selling mistakes and can use a refresher on how to avoid them in the future. Would you be available on April 3 at 4 p.m. to speak at our event?

PS: Thanks for your interest in speaking to our group!

Sound too simple? Well, sometimes it works this way. I can't guarantee that this kind of response will float in every time, but I'll certainly predict that if you send out enough of these e-mail inquiries to truly targeted groups, you'll indeed begin hearing from them. And that's the first step in getting through the door. Think of it as a numbers game: your odds increase with every e-mail inquiry you send out.

THOUGHT NOTES

What about Speakers' Bureaus?

Speakers' bureaus can be effective in obtaining speaking engagements, as that's precisely the business they are in:

matching speakers with speaking opportunities. They will be most helpful, however, if (1) you have written a book, especially one that is of interest to a specific audience, (2) you already speak a lot each year, especially to large audiences, and/or (3) you already earn high fees from your speaking engagements.

Bureaus take a healthy percentage of each fee, typically 30 to 40 percent, so they depend upon your natural market value; they won't spend time coaching you to get started or working on your behalf to "develop" you. As a result, don't look to a bureau to function as your mentor or manager. If you are lucky enough to have a bureau put you on its list, you'll still need to promote yourself through articles, books, media, and other methods in order to create a demand for your speaking topics. Therefore, signing up with a speaker's bureau does not absolve you from the need to actively practice thoughtleading.

Fees

As with publishing articles, when you begin this process, fees should be the farthest thing from your mind. The value to you of speaking to groups is to spread the good word about you the expert to prospects, influencers, colleagues, and anyone else who might pass your name around. This means that at first, pro bono speaking will be a regular format for you. Of course, it doesn't hurt to put an actual dollar value on your speaking availability, even if you're more than willing to reduce this amount or waive it as circumstances apply. When someone invites you to speak to a group, for example, you first might ask (1) what will be the profile of the attendees? and (2) does the group have a budget to work with?

If the answer to the second question is yes, we do have a budget, tell the planner that your standard speaking fee is $2,500 (or whatever you're comfortable with) plus expenses, then wait to see if he or she blinks. Maybe you'll get lucky and the planner will say, "Sure, we could afford that." If so, answer calmly, "That will be acceptable." Then go nuts after you hang up the phone!

More frequently, though, the response is likely to be, "Well, that might be a little stiff for us" or "Ah, well, we don't actually have a budget for speaker fees."

If the response to (1) indicates that the audience will clearly be a good one for you, representing your target audience, for example, then find a way to do the gig anyway. But don't just lower your fee, as that would suggest that you weren't that valuable in the first place. Instead say, "Well, it sounds like a good group you have there, and I do offer a few pro bono talks every year, so I'll be happy to come down. But I would appreciate it if you can cover my expenses and if I can bring along my assistant (or wife or business partner) at no charge." Make the group give you something in return, and be prepared with a list of possible counterrequests that you can work from. That way it will be a true and fair exchange, as it should be, not just a giveaway.

Common Speaking Mistakes

One big mistake that many new speakers make is giving in to a fear that their presentation will be too subtle, that it will "give away the store" without yielding them, in the end, new prospects and new business. So they turn their presentation into a blatant advertisement for their services, beating people over the head with the idea that they should buy the speaker's products or services. Of course, the opposite is true: only by generating trust and eliminating pressure will most speakers succeed in coaxing new customers out of their audience. The hard sell, on the other hand, typically sends prospects racing for the door.

What other mistakes do beginning speakers (and some veterans too) commonly make? Let's ask thoughtleader Suzanne Bates this question, as she covers this and other issues in her book of gold *Speak Like a CEO: Secrets of Commanding Attention and Getting Results*

(McGraw-Hill). In this excerpt, Bates cites eight particularly egregious mistakes that smart, seasoned speakers have learned to avoid:

> *Denise had just won a big promotion. She was not someone who typically sought the limelight or asked for help. So Denise spent the first weeks working alone, avoiding presentations and even speaking up in meetings (unless directly spoken to). When asked to make a PowerPoint presentation, she panicked.*
>
> *A crisis is not a good time to learn how to make an effective presentation. Denise quickly put together 20 slides, prepared some points, and practiced answering potential questions. After pulling an all-nighter Denise delivered an adequate speech while learning an invaluable lesson: You don't have to be a perfect speaker to be successful, but you must be prepared.*
>
> *This is the true distinction between success and failure in public speaking. To ensure that lack of preparation won't be your downfall when you take to the podium, consider these most common mistakes budding public speakers often make.*

Mistake 1: Underestimating the Importance of Public Speaking to Your Career

> *A retail executive with a strong financial background and track record was promoted to CFO. In the first weeks, she uncovered problems in her operation and quietly went to work, never seeking the limelight nor help. While that approach may have worked in the past, it was about to backfire. Senior leaders were expected to help each other by sharing information. Emails leaked out about her problematic situation and the senior team confronted her. The CEO scheduled a meeting and she was asked to make a PowerPoint presentation.*
>
> *The new executive not only had to put together her slides and prepare her talk; she knew she had to get ready to*

face some tough questions. Fortunately she pulled a lot of people in to help. She practiced, prepared and delivered a decent presentation.

If you want to lead the company, you should never underestimate the importance of public speaking. You will be judged by the way you handle the hot seat. Judgment Day isn't six months before they decide to make you CEO. Judgment days are all along the way. You have to be ready long before you have to be ready.

Mistake 2: "Winging" Important Speeches

Eric, a vice-president regarded as the candidate to succeed the CEO, was asked to deliver a presentation to the company's leadership group. Buried under several other projects, Eric figured he could probably wing it. Bad idea!

What made matters worse was that the same day Eric was to speak, a colleague named Fred gave a great presentation. Fred had done his homework, organizing his thinking, and practicing the night before. In contrast to Eric, Fred appeared cool, well organized, polished and he answered questions with ease.

Even if you feel generally comfortable in front of an audience, winging your presentation will usually prove to be a huge mistake. Your talk must be organized and your points delivered crisply. Otherwise, the effect could be less than your audience expects, harming your competent, professional image.

Mistake 3: Leaving It All to a Speechwriter

If you can hire a good speechwriter, you should. Every speaker can use someone to sketch out ideas, brainstorm and find ways to improve on what you have to say. But don't let your speechwriter do it all.

In the end, you must be comfortable and familiar with what you're going to say. Your speechwriter won't be behind that podium when the big day comes . . . you will. Let your speechwriter give you some help but the presentation will be yours, so make it yours.

Mistake 4: Not Answering the Question

Be ready and willing to honestly answer the toughest questions head on. If you don't know the answer, say so: "I'm sorry but I just do not know" or "I'll have to look into that." It may not be the ideal spot to be in, but getting caught later in a lie is much worse for your reputation. Your audience will appreciate the truth.

Mistake 5: Forgetting Your Audience

Those who attend your presentation are often leaving piles of work on their desks to come and hear you talk. You cannot give them that time back, you can only thank them for giving it to you and then do your best to make it worth their while.

Whether speaking to executive officers, your staff, or even job candidates, think first about who they are and what they want to know, even before you write down the opening words of your speech. If you're not sure, interview a handful of people who will be in your audience. Find out what they need to learn. Remember your audience, and chances are they'll remember you.

Mistake 6: Blowing the Easy Questions

In their frenzy to study up on the difficult questions, many speakers end up unprepared for the slam-dunk ones. Yet if they fumble these, they'll look as unprepared as ever. Rather than seeming knowledgeable, they'll convey the reverse. "How can he not know THAT?!" So don't forget the potential softball questions as well as the hard.

Mistake 7: Not Knowing When to Fold 'em

Ever had to sit through a wedding toast that just kept going and going and going? That's because time flies when you are in the spotlight and what seems like only a few moments to a novice speaker is actually many minutes.

To be sure you don't make this mistake, time your speech by standing up as you mock-deliver it. Do not time it by sitting and reading it because this takes less time. Speak out loud.

And be ready to improvise by tuning into your crowd. Sometimes things are running behind schedule and an audience may be getting restless for a break, signaling you to cut your talk even shorter. Lincoln's Gettysburg address was less than two minutes long. Remember, few are ever criticized for giving a speech that was too brief.

Mistake 8: Not Having Fun

Humor helps connect you to your audience. You don't have to be David Letterman. Just try to have a little fun. Tell a quick story that's amusing, make a light-hearted remark about the commute in or the weather. Humor will warm up your audience.

In summary, everyone makes mistakes in public speaking. The key is to identify a lesson learned and try to correct it your next time out. If these eight common mistakes help you better avoid such gaffes, all the better. Keep speaking, keep practicing, keep preparing and before long, mistakes like these will be a thing of the past.

THOUGHT NOTES

Feedback and Evaluations

My old friend freelance writer Gary Provost was also an accomplished and popular writing teacher who regarded feedback as generally unhelpful. "Invariably, half the people will tell you the room was too hot," he used to say, "while the other half will tell you it was too cold!"

Some speakers feel the need for feedback; others loathe it, especially when it is unsolicited. Some speakers feel that feedback helps them get better; others feel that it rarely tells them anything they didn't already know. Generally you will know if you did well or badly by the feeling in the room when you are done, although there may be specifics about your performance that feedback could help identify.

I once gave a talk on thoughtleading to the Institute of Management Consultants chapter in Princeton, New Jersey, using a format that I had followed dozens of times before. But afterwards, a few attendees wrote on the evaluations that they wished I had given a few concrete examples of thoughtleaders (as I provided in the first two chapters of this book), including how their thoughtleading lifestyles developed. I took the feedback to heart and incorporated such a section in my next presentation, to a senior executives association in Massachusetts. The new material seemed to round out my overall explanation of how thoughtleading transforms an expert into a specialist with an edge.

A Word about PowerPoint

At a speaking gig in Pennsylvania, I did my usual thing, which typically involves just talking to and interacting with my audience without the aid of charts or slides or overheads. After I finished, one attendee thanked me profusely "for *not* using PowerPoint."

When PPT first came on the scene, it seemed that everybody had to include a PPT component in their presentations. And, of course, as the bells and whistles developed, the PPT parts got glitzier and glitzier. After a while, the whole thing got way out of control.

Today, it seems that those of us who have stayed away from PowerPoint have been declared the winners. The large number of poorly done PPT presentations has given birth to a resistance movement to PowerPoint presentations.

In fact Tom Kennedy, founder and president of the Kennedy Group, a speech coaching consultancy in the Boston area, actually refers to the PPT phenomenon as "Death by PowerPoint." He recommends giving up slides altogether, or if you don't feel ready for that, he says, try putting your presentation together first, without choosing slides, then carefully take note of whether adding slides will help or hurt you. "If it's not truly a visual aid," he says, "it's your competition!"

So stay away from PPT slides if you can and practice speaking "without a net." You'll learn to communicate more directly with your audience, more clearly, more spontaneously, and more comfortably. You'll stop fearing public speaking, and you'll look forward to any chance to share your thoughtleading ideas and show off your expert's edge.

10

Pillar 3: Keeping Your Edge with Fresh Thinking

Be curious about ideas.

Marie Curie

Practitioners of thoughtleading think great thoughts. When you are practicing thoughtleading, your ideas evolve and are developed. When you are practicing thoughtleading, you reevaluate your assumptions, stretch your thinking in new and original directions, and open up your mind to "fresh thinking."

To ensure that fresh thinking is indeed fresh, it makes sense to search out unexpected notions and information from time to time by asking survey questions, compiling data, and learning what others believe and think. In other words, conduct some original research.

Michael Norris, senior analyst at Simba Information, cites three benefits in particular that conducting original research will deliver to the expert seeking an edge:

1. *Long-term value.* "Part of the reason a lot of companies and consultants don't bother conducting original research," Norris says, "is that they are deterred by the amount of time and money involved up front. Even a modest research study can raise the specter of an enormous interruption in day-to-day business flow."

   Yet research projects can pay dividends, he explains, for months or even years after they've been completed. Though the life expectancy of information, especially these days, can be relatively short, the attention that a new study can attract may be both priceless at the beginning and capable of contributing residual effects way down the road. For example, the initial Atkins Diet research on the effect of carbohydrates on the body continues to have repercussions today, 40 years later, despite the untimely death of Dr. Robert Atkins in 2003.

2. *No one else has it.* Since so few individuals and firms go this extra step, your reputation as a fresh thinker will surely drive your attractiveness up a notch. Although you may already be the go-to authority in your area of expertise, the fact that you are doing this research will help you stand out even more. Not only do you know what you're talking about, but you have information that even competing experts do not have. You are the expert that people would be crazy not to turn to every time!

3. *It's thoughtleading money in the bank.* Once you've amassed original data on a topic, its possibilities for expanding your reputation as a thoughtleader are truly endless. A few examples:
   - Your fresh data can be spotlighted on your Web site and in other marketing collateral.
   - You can build a book and a series of articles around your findings.
   - You can deliver presentations based on your findings.
   - You can strategically incorporate your unique fresh data into sales calls and prospect presentations.

- You can distribute summaries of your findings to both news media and industry analysts.
- You can sell your research as a product, charging a hefty fee for the executive summary and/or the entire study.

Looking at these benefits, you can see how the investment of even large amounts of time, energy, and money in a research project can return dividends. True thoughtleaders will recognize this, while their competition will hang back, doubting, or unaware of, the obvious benefits.

Traits of Successful Researchers

Before getting started, it's helpful to understand what qualities make for a successful research project. According to Leonard Fuld, perhaps the world's leading thoughtleader in the area of competitive intelligence, these qualities should be part of a profile of the "smart researcher." He cites four traits as being common to such a profile.

Having written four books on the subject and having founded from scratch one of the world's most respected competitive intelligence-gathering firms (Fuld & Company, headquartered in Cambridge, Massachusetts), Fuld knows what he's talking about. In his now-classic first book, *Competitive Intelligence: How to Get It, How to Use It* (Wiley), he lists the four traits of a successful researcher:

1. *Insight.* "Know your sources before beginning the assignment," Fuld writes. "Understand which sources might help or speed up the research process. . . . Insight allows you to save time and begin probing . . . almost immediately, without wasting time."

2. *Creativity.* When basic sources fail, Fuld says, the smart researcher "will uncover new sources to address the problem." Use your imagination and keep looking for someone who can answer all your questions.

3. *Strategy.* To save precious time, especially with a fast-approaching deadline, "the astute researcher will devise a plan of attack, a means to efficiently find the vital intelligence. Random research means wasted time, lost dollars, and failure to meet deadlines."

4. *Persistence.* "Where all else fails, keep trying." All too often, Fuld explains, someone will tell you that no one has that information. Just as often, he says, "you can bet that someone surely does. Countless projects were solved because the researcher tried just one more contact, made just one additional phone call."

Boiling down these traits, it appears that successful researchers rely on preparedness, resourcefulness, persistence, and innovation. Believing that the data you seek can be found and never losing sight of that belief is the key to concluding your research with valuable new thoughtleading data in hand.

Getting Started: Objectives

The largest question to resolve before beginning your research project may be the most obvious one: what are your objectives? Simba's Michael Norris advises crystallizing your objectives by answering three simple but crucial questions:

- What do you want to know?
- What do you want to ask?
- Where do you want to look for the answers?

The first two questions should be answered internally. It's entirely up to you to decide the focus of the knowledge that your research will pursue and the questions you must ask in order to recognize that you have found that knowledge.

The third question involves external sources, perhaps derived partly from secondary sources such as books and articles, but probably coming more from such primary sources as knowledgeable individuals and people who are intimately involved with the problem being studied. One often overlooked way to locate such individuals is to approach a professional association that represents your target interviewees.

For example, a survey targeting human resources executives might be undertaken through SHRM, the Society for Human Resource Management.

If, on the other hand, you are targeting manufacturing executives, you might approach the Association of Industrial Managers, the American Manufacturing Institute, or the National Association of Manufacturers.

Newspaper editors? Try the American Society of Newspaper Editors and the World Association of Newspapers.

Chemical waste plant managers? There's the National Association of Chemical Distributors and the Air & Waste Management Association.

As you may recall from my chapter on speaking, associations exist for every cluster of professionals imaginable. Seek them out via the Internet or a directory of professional associations, which you can find in your local library. You may even be able to partner with an association, or at least gain some assistance from it, so that you can carry out your research with a minimum of time wasted scurrying about trying to find an individual here and there to interview.

Getting Started II: Overcoming Challenges

Bruce Katcher, Ph.D., is president of Discovery Surveys, Inc., a firm that helps organizations reduce employee turnover by conducting high-quality surveys to track and improve company relationships with employees and customers. Author of 30 *Reasons Employees Hate Their Managers* (AMACOM Books), Katcher suggests a nine-step approach for overcoming challenges faced by researchers new to the game.

In your quest to become a thoughtleader, he explains, conducting research studies is a sure-fire, time-tested approach for getting there. In the beginning, however, you will be facing some challenges, including:

- You may never have conducted research before.
- You likely have lots of highly credible competitors.
- You may have little, if any, money to invest.

Fret not! Here is Katcher's nine-step approach to maximize your chances of early research success.

Step 1: Set Clear Objectives

Be clear on why are you conducting the research. It's not because you're curious or want to change the world; it's because you are trying to increase your credibility in the marketplace and sell more products or services. It therefore doesn't have to be research that's published in a refereed technical journal or that appears in the *Wall Street Journal*. It merely has to help promote your professional goals.

Step 2: Select an Appropriate Topic

You next need to select an "appropriate" research topic. Let's say that you're a professional meeting planner, trying to launch a consulting business specializing in helping health sciences associations manage and run their meetings. Your target market is professional meeting planners employed by healthcare organizations.

Your goal is to establish credibility and visibility with this group, so you need to choose a topic that meeting planners will be interested in learning about and will be willing to be interviewed for. Most importantly, it needs to be a topic that will help you ingratiate yourself with them.

You are aware that meeting planners are always interested in saving money and you would love to establish yourself as the go-to authority that can help them reduce costs. There's your topic: "How meeting planners in the healthcare industry reduce their meeting costs."

Step 3: Find a Credible Source for Your Results

Next you must find a credible publication, read by meeting planners, that would likely publish the results of your yet-to-be-conducted research study. Or, find a professional association of meeting planners that would like you to report the study results at one of their upcoming meetings. Having this in your back pocket will enable you to more easily recruit participants for your study.

Step 4: Develop the Survey

Without getting into all of the technicalities of survey development, here are three general guidelines for actually developing your survey:

1. Keep your questionnaire short.
2. Make certain you gather information that will be valuable to your target market (and that will enable you to write an interesting report).
3. Include both open- and closed-ended questions. Responses to closed-ended questions will enable you to cite statistics when you report on the results. Open-ended responses will provide you with a greater depth of understanding.

Step 5: Procure a List of Prospects

You will need access to a list of potential respondents. Ideally, the participants will be prospects for your consulting services. If you are going to conduct an interview study, you will need their telephone numbers. If you are going to conduct a paper survey, you will need their mailing addresses. If you are going to conduct a Web-based survey, you will need e-mail addresses.

Step 6: Conduct the Survey

My suggestion here is a telephone interview survey. This would enable you to actually speak with your prospects. However, paper or electronic surveys have their advantages as well, as they can provide you with greater precision while not requiring as much of your time. Surveys like paper surveys, however, often incur greater out-of-pocket expenses than telephone surveys.

Note: Before conducting your survey, let your potential participants know that the results will be published and/or presented at an upcoming professional meeting. For their participation, reward them with a special complimentary executive summary.

Step 7: Follow up with Participants

After collecting the data, analyze it and pick out the major themes you will write about. Then write up an executive summary and send it out to all participants. Follow up later to see if they have any questions, too. The more "touches" you can create with these prospects, the better. After all, they are potential clients!

Step 8: Publish and/or Present the Results

Follow through on your plan to publish and/or present the results. Send published articles and reports to the participants and to your prospects.

Step 9: Leverage Your Survey Results

Now that you have results in hand, you are the definitive expert on this particular topic. In addition to your planned articles and presentations, do the following:

1. Send out a press release or two (or three) about the study.
2. Post the report on your website and in your e-letters.

3. Make sure your clients and prospects can easily download the report from your website.
4. Include your Executive Summary in all packets of information you send out to prospects.
5. Include your Executive Summary in your proposals to prospects as well.

Many people forget that the results of their surveys can be utilized in many ways to establish and maintain higher credibility in their field and within their target markets. Once you get really good at this, you might even consider charging clients and prospects for your reports. At that point, your research thoughtleader star will have risen dramatically.

THOUGHT NOTES

Henry David Thoreau Said It Well: "Simplify, Simplify!"

How do you begin to put excitement back into your company? How do you regain not only relevance but the feeling that you are *essential* to your customers? How do you know if you are still delivering real value to your customers? This is the easy part: you ask them. If you face flat sales and high customer churn, it's probably because you've lost touch with your customers. Just ask them; it's that simple, and they'll tell you what they want. Survey them, ask them, talk to them. They'll tell you how to sell to them, too. Your customers know perfectly well how you can reinvent your company to meet their needs.

—Shelley Hall, President,
Catalytic Management Group

When Conducting Interviews

The actual process of conducting original research often involves not just questionnaires but face-to-face or voice-to-voice interviews as well. Positioning and branding expert Michael Antman, president of McSweeney & Antman, explains it this way: "The most effective research isn't necessarily the most rigidly designed. In fact, a so-called loosely designed program—whether qualitative or quantitative—may not appear very scientific at first glance, yet sometimes it will reveal more real truths than the most carefully crafted and comprehensive research programs."

Michael Antman's thesis, with which I concur, is derived from the fact that our human brains are both complex and quirky. Therefore, tightly designed surveys that attempt to squeeze every interviewee into the same mold can frequently result in lost opportunities. Never deviating from a specific set of questions runs the risk of failing to give respondents enough latitude to expand on their answers. Your results may then seem solidly scientific, but they could end up yielding only a limited understanding of your research topic.

"Rigidly designed research doesn't allow anything to fall between the cracks . . . because there are no cracks," Antman says. "Yet it is the stray answer, the unexpected insight, and the uncategorizable response that often create the greatest opportunity for genuine insight on the part of the marketing professional."

Want to be sure that your qualitative interviews stay that way— that is, qualitative? Try these five suggestions from an article that Antman published in *MarketingProfs*:

1. *Put away your questions.* Put away your questions once the interview starts, attempting instead to simply engage your interviewees in a conversation about the topic area. Near the end of the interview, pull out your list and see if there are any questions that you want to be sure you cover before you leave.

   To which I would add: in this age of e-mail, you have no worries! You can always e-mail a follow-up question or two now that you've cemented a bond with your interviewee. This will probably yield not merely the answer to a question that you forgot to ask but a few afterthought gems that your interviewee also forgot to include.

2. *Start at the front lines.* Begin your research in earnest by speaking with people on the front lines of an organization—perhaps, for example, the salespeople—before you head either outward (to the target market) or upward (to the C Suite). This gives you the freedom, Antman explains, to ask fairly basic questions without worrying about wasting the time of senior executives or busy customers. "It's not that front-line personnel have a lot of time either, but most of them are flattered to be asked about their jobs by someone who seems to really care about their answers." So front-liners become the best place to begin.

3. *Leave your image at home.* To be effective, a research process must never, at any stage, be about you, the interviewer. Yet many researchers worry about looking "uninformed" as they ask their questions. Doing this leads you to lose sight of why you are there in the first place, i.e., to acquire information! "Sometimes the most elementary questions, the sort that others fail to ask because 'everyone knows the answer,' are those that yield the most surprising responses."

   To which I would add: Research is about information gathering and insight gathering as well. It may involve hearing what you already know straight from the horse's mouth. You may learn about something in a new way, or you may just acquire a quote that says it more authentically than you can.

   Years ago, in my freelance reporter days, I used to ask what I came to call "stupid reporter questions" in every interview. These might be questions that I knew the answer to very well but that I wanted to hear articulated by my interviewee. If I looked stupid while asking a question, so be it. I knew that if I walked away with some terrific unique quotes, I'd end up looking a whole lot smarter to those who read my finished article.

And throughout hundreds of interviews and thousands of such stupid reporter questions, never once did an interviewee respond, "Oh, come on, you know the answer to that." Instead, every single time the person simply leaped forward to answer the question.

4. *Shut up already.* Should an interviewee rattle off what sounds like a canned response, try doing something that's extremely hard to do: shut up. In fact, shut up for an uncomfortable number of seconds, as if you really don't quite understand what you just heard. This sometimes forces a shy, inexperienced, or downright resistant respondent to get real. More often than not, your interviewee will break the silence by offering something additional and more natural.

5. *Ask, "Have I missed anything?"* The purpose of a qualitative interview is to tease as much information out of your interviewee as you can, so as your time nears its conclusion, ask: "Have I missed anything?" or: "What other questions *should* I have asked?" Or this one: "Before we finish, what could you add to what we've been discussing today?" If you don't ask such questions, your respondent will probably not tell you this additional information. As the interviewer, you are the discussion leader. Do your job by asking any and all questions that will help draw your interviewee out. And understand that your job doesn't end until you hang up the phone or leave the interviewee's building.

The Lowdown on Surveys

You'll also want to consider conducting a survey as a means of gathering your research data. The trick here is doing so in a way that collects the opinions you need without alienating your surveyees. Brian Henderson, a marketing thoughtleader with Prezza Technologies, reminds people in his widely published article "Twelve Tips for Conducting Effective Surveys" that, "We've all been on the receiving end of far too many poorly constructed surveys that required too much time and energy simply to share our thoughts." When we encounter 10- or 20-page surveys, it's easy to assume that the value of our time was not taken into consideration by the survey's designers.

Don't you make this same mistake! To help you avoid doing so, here are 12 seasoned tips from Henderson on how to survey effectively without simultaneously pushing your surveyees away:

1. *Define the survey's purpose.* Figure out exactly what you want your customers to tell you. For instance, you may want to find out whether they are satisfied with your service. So ask them. Do not gather any extra data if you aren't sure exactly what you are going to do with the results.

2. *Keep it short and sweet.* It shouldn't take a respondent more than ten minutes to complete a questionnaire. Make it five or even two minutes or less, if you can manage. Also, keep survey respondents in the loop along the way by telling them up front how long the survey might take, including a progress bar and maybe even naming the survey in a way that indicates how long it will take, for example, "My 3-minute poll."

    Time is a top complaint among people who have taken surveys, so address this objection immediately and move past it.

3. *Keep it simple.* Make sure that respondents will understand the questions. Don't use jargon and don't make the questions too complex. Make sure that the questions are not worded for "insiders." Americanized clichés and catchphrases do not work overseas and can be embarrassing. Acronyms will quickly turn off those who do not know the meaning of the acronym.

4. *Save demographic questions for last.* Keep information that is less crucial to your surveys toward the end, or else people

will be apt to lose interest in your survey. Also, when you are asking for personal information, make sure you have a privacy policy that is easily visible, and abide by it. Recent news reports of company data losses have made Internet users even more skeptical than ever.

5. *Keep it specific.* If you are conducting surveys of large audiences, don't ask open-ended questions that will give you a wide range of answers. That will make it difficult to analyze the results. Questions should be either yes/no or multiple choice.

6. *Make it consistent.* If the first question asks your respondents to rate your customer service on a scale of 1 to 5, with 5 being highly satisfactory, make sure that in subsequent questions 5 always corresponds to being highly satisfactory.

    Although people may be inclined to move through the survey faster as a result, it is better than having them choose the wrong answer by mistake.

7. *Follow logic.* Make sure that one question leads naturally into another. Usually, the first questions will be broad and the follow-up ones will be more specific. You would not start out by asking, "Why don't you like Professor Greenwall?" This is too specific, and it's a leading question.

    You first need to find out whether the survey respondent has positive or negative feelings about the professor, and then ask why he is not liked.

8. *Do a test.* Give the survey first to a group of employees or customers. Doing so will tell you how long the survey takes to complete and whether any questions are confusing. This testing is extremely important and gets overlooked far too often.

    Those who are focused on a survey project begin to get so connected to the project that they can lose track of minor details. Other people can bring fresh insight and ideas and catch embarrassing mistakes before they go out to a large audience.

9. *Avoid weekends.* Best practices of e-mail marketing apply here. The best time to send e-mail to workers is between Tuesday and Thursday during a normal business week. E-mails sent on a Monday or a Friday are likely to be put off until later, and by then you've lost the audience's immediate attention.

10. *Send reminders.* If you e-mail the survey, set a deadline to receive the results. Make sure you give people plenty of time to answer the survey. A few days before, send a reminder. Some software packages will allow you to automate the sending of e-mails and personalize the note using mail merge.

11. *Entice.* Give your customers a good reason to answer your survey. Offer them a discount or give them a gift certificate. You're asking them to do you a favor, so show your appreciation. Make sure the incentive is somewhat relevant to the customer's interests. You wouldn't give away an extreme-sports vacation to someone who would rather watch them on TV.

12. *Share.* Last, but not least, share the results with your customers and let them know what action you will take. If you need more information, do follow-up surveys. But remember, you're asking them to take the time to help you, so be careful not to abuse that relationship.

Hopefully, these tips will help those who are relatively new at conducting surveys to make fewer mistakes when they attempt to solicit professional feedback for their business.

Should You Hire a Researcher?

Hiring a researcher or a research firm when you finally feel ready to launch your first research project is not a bad idea. In fact, it's probably a darned good idea. Not only can conducting original research be time consuming, but a real pro can also save you from the steep learning curve of trying to do it right. Also, it doesn't hurt to include a seasoned analytical eye when the time comes for drawing your conclusions and translating them into insights.

Hiring the right research firm can, of course, be a daunting endeavor if you've never done it before. So here are a few tips from Garry Upton, executive vice president of client service at Decision Analyst Inc., based on his article "What You Should Know before Calling a Researcher," also published on the Web site *MarketingProfs*.

Like many of us, Upton writes, researchers lead inordinately harried lives. It is therefore critical, he explains, that you and the researcher are on the same page about your wants and needs. Here are his tips for ensuring that this happens.

When initially calling a researcher, Upton writes, "take a few minutes to relate the call's background, i.e., why you and/or your associates believe research is required. As you describe your needs, add any information that might help the researcher understand your objectives. For example, does this study need to be conducted every year? Frequency significantly affects how a research project's design must be formulated."

Also, Upton says, review other information that might be used in combination with the study. This additional information (internal data, earlier studies, and other such things) will help your researcher design the data files (cross-tabulations) produced for the analysis. In all cases, share only as much as you are comfortable sharing. Realize, however, that the more you share, the better the subsequent research will be.

Objectives and Methodologies

To help you best achieve your goal, researchers need to understand what your objectives are. In your initial conversation with the research professional, feel free to suggest methodologies while remaining open to alternative techniques. Spend a few minutes discussing and better understanding the ways in which the use of different methodologies may expand or reduce the overall usefulness of the study. You need to make certain that you understand why your researcher is suggesting certain methodologies, Upton explains.

Budget

Being open about your budget helps researchers with the overall study design. You may not be comfortable sharing your budget, but at least you should try not to ask for more research help than you think you can afford. Remember, purchasing research is like acquiring a new car: a less expensive one might still get you to your destination, even if not quite as quickly, dependably, or comfortably as a pricier model.

To summarize, nothing substitutes for professional marketing research when the time comes to uncover new trends or new industry data, Upton insists. Entering into the process blindly, however, can cause you problems. So take a little time to prepare. Once you do, original research will not only prove beneficial to your bottom line, but may open up a whole new world for you to exploit and explore.

All Over for Libraries?

Is it all over for libraries? We all love the idea of visiting our local library, walking confidently up to the reference desk and asking the research librarian for a certain book category, and then being directed within seconds or minutes to the exact spot in the library where you can find what you're looking for. This is how it works, right? It's so simple, so complete, so comforting, so predictable. It's a safe and helpful place, the library.

Yet while researching this chapter in a Boston library, I encountered something quite different.

My adventure began when I left my writing table on the library's third floor and moseyed downstairs to a bank of desktops occupied by other library patrons who were merrily clicking into the library database. They seemed to be searching for book titles in the online catalog, which is what I wanted to do.

But my efforts always seemed to bring me to the Internet, not the catalog, so, efficient dude that I am, I gave up after only a few minutes and strode over to the nearby reference desk. I'd been seeing this librarian—let's call her June—sitting there for years; she was a true veteran of the place who would surely know at once where to find books on research, which was what I was seeking. She probably would not even need to look it up. After all, if an experienced research librarian didn't know where to find books on research, who would?

Her phone rang just as I reached her. She picked it right up, giving me a slight wink as if to say, "Don't worry, this'll only take a sec." Then she proceeded to hang in there with the caller for some minutes.

Bored, I strayed away from the front of her desk for an instant, which let another patron, oblivious to my even standing there, brush right past me and take up my "spot." Oh, heck, I thought, this is getting me nowhere. I decided to go away and try something else.

Back upstairs at my writing table, I decided to try the library computers again, this time one that was only two tables away from where I had been sitting. Why hadn't I started here in the first place?

Filling in the topic field with "research methods," I came up with a few titles, but none of them told me where to go to find the books I wanted. After punching around a bit to figure this out, and getting nowhere, I scouted out a volunteer I'd been seeing in the area for weeks, always carefully restocking books on all the nearby shelves.

Why not turn to the nearest "go-to" authority? I thought. After all, she's here day in and day out. Surely she would know which shelves held the books on research.

At first, my question bewildered her. Then she asked, "What kind of research? Any area in particular?"

Ah, spoken like a true consultant, I thought. First find out what the client is looking for, then go help. "Just general or basic books on research methodology," I replied, confident that I was now in the best of hands.

"Hmm," she murmured. "Let's see." She led me back to the very place where I had been sitting at my table and started scanning the shelves there. "There may be some books on research here," she said.

Unfortunately, I knew otherwise. I'd been idly glancing at those very shelves for weeks now. I knew almost all of them like the back of my hands.

"You know, I'm really not sure where research books would be," the volunteer finally sighed. Then in a burst of inspiration she said: "Let's try the online catalog."

Plunking herself down at the same computer screen I'd just been scrutinizing, she started clicking away. At least an expert was sitting there now, I thought.

After a minute or so, however, she seemed as beaten as I was.

"Hmmm . . . they don't seem to be coming up." A few minutes more and she threw up her hands. "Maybe you should go down and see June," she said. "She's the research librarian; she'll know what to do."

OK, then. I thanked her kindly and decided, what the heck, maybe June would be free now. So I skipped down the two flights to see her again, and lo and behold—yes, she was free! Now I would really get somewhere.

"Hi, June, I'm looking for books on research methodology," I said. "I thought you might point me to some place in the stacks where they might all be."

"What kind of research?" she asked.

"Oh, just your basic research," I said. "Research methodology, how to research, that kind of thing."

"OK," she said intently, turning to click at her screen. For many seconds, however, she stared somberly at it, saying nothing. Finally she said, "It's running very slow today; let me switch to this other screen." So she moved over to a second screen at her desk, then started clicking away again.

Things there moved more slowly still. "Sorry, the system's running very slowly today all over," she apologized.

Then, all of a sudden she exclaimed, "OK, here's one. . . . I found something for you." Then she added, "Although it's from 1986. Things in research have changed since then."

Yes, I thought, they certainly have.

So June clicked around some more. "OK, here's something else; this one might be good for you." While writing down the library number for me, she mentioned that this book focused on fiction research. "Probably not what you're looking for," she said, hoping to be wrong. Well, no, June, sorry, not at all.

"OK, OK, here's another one; this one might be good . . ." Then, before she could tell me, her phone rang! "Hello, Reference Desk," she said, starting to take down what the caller was saying. All hope, I thought to myself, was about to be lost. Thankfully, however, I then heard June say, "OK, can I call you back in a few minutes? I have someone here I'm in the middle of helping."

Hanging up, June was back on the case. "OK, OK, here's a book called *The Complete Idiot's Guide to Research*," she said.

"Perfect," I replied, truly feeling that way.

"The only thing is," she added, "we don't have it here. But we can order it for you."

I sighed to myself, but to June I replied as nicely as pie, "Sure, why not? I'd love to see it."

"OK," she said, excitedly. "Do you have your library card?" Ulp, well, I did have one, but it was back upstairs at my table on the third floor.

"OK, OK, that's all right," June said, "just let me look you up here." Her computer was now doing its job well, finding my information without making me trudge back upstairs for my plastic library card.

"OK," June said now, triumphantly. "You're all set. We'll call you when it comes in."

"How long will that take?" I asked, quietly fearful.

"Oh, just a few days," she answered. So as not to accomplish nothing that day, before I left, I decided to ask June about that other book that she had found previously, the one from 1986.

"Oh, yes," she said, writing out a number for me. "It's up there on the reference balcony," she said, pointing up to a second floor tier above us. I thanked her and bounced upstairs. At least I would take a look at some kind of research book today, the only one, in fact, that June had been able to find that was physically present.

When I located it, however, it was not exactly the kind of book I had been looking for, but it was worth the trip for its irony alone. The title of the book was A *Guide to Library Research Methods*!

Mine for the Taking

I had just spent 40 minutes on this. In contrast, when I went back to my table, I clicked open my browser and Googled "research methodology books." A lengthy list of books and resources for such books came up in a flash, including quite a few that I knew I would love to take a good look at.

But since I couldn't, I next Googled "research methodology articles." A few minutes of browsing time later, I was again staring at a lengthy list, this time of articles and resources for articles on research. One of them was exactly what I was looking for, so I clicked on its Web site. After a couple of minutes setting myself up for membership, bingo, I was in! All the information that I had been longing for lay right before me, mine for the taking.

Within minutes I had three suitable articles to use as references for this chapter, which I settled back to read. Total elapsed time: 10 minutes tops. The results had come to me without my leaving my table, without my asking for anyone else's help, without watching the clock slip, slip away as dead ends popped up and down all around me.

Yes, it may be all over for libraries.

Ongoing Inquiry

Thoughtleaders don't simply regurgitate age-old notions, they turn them on their ears and examine them from new angles. Every individual on our planet has a unique perspective that original research serves to test and confirm or refute, and possibly transform. When thoughtleaders commit themselves to this kind of ongoing inquiry, fresh thinking results and the thoughtleader's knowledge, interpretation, and practices evolve. This permits true thoughtleading to take place.

Thought Notes

Reflections on a Research Project

In 2006, Carol Bergeron, founder and president of Bergeron Associates, a human capital management and organizational performance improvement consulting firm, partnered with Insight Management Group, experts in project management and change management, to conduct a study of C-level executive views on enterprise performance, using both a Web-based survey and one-on-one interviews. Over 100 executives participated, representing 20 states and 3 countries. Over 100 questions examined their views and practices on enterprise performance. Carol reflects on the experience:

1. *What primarily motivated you to undertake an original research project?*
   Conducting original research is a great way to gain insight on issues important to your clients so that you can better understand and serve them.
2. *What benefits did you derive from conducting your CEO survey?*
   It was an effective way of building professional relationships with a broader group of CEOs. Also, publishing and disseminating our research results helped with branding, establishing my firm as a credible, visible source of valuable insight in the business community.

   In terms of thoughtleading actions, the survey helped me get more articles published since publishers love articles based on original research. You can also integrate research results with everything else you do as a thoughtleader: your presentations, your articles, your newsletters, your conversations.

3. *Was there a downside to conducting a research project?*
   Conducting a research project is a very time-consuming undertaking and taps into every skill and competence you have (and don't have).

4. *Would you do anything differently should you undertake a research survey again?*
   The next time, and yes there will be a next time, I will partner with a research/educational institution or professional association. Recruiting survey participants was more challenging than expected. Partnering with an organization that has an established client or contact base would have made that challenge a lot easier.

11

Pillar 4: Creatively
Leveraging the Internet

Ideas won't keep. Something must be done about them.

ALFRED NORTH WHITEHEAD

IT RUNS TOTALLY AGAINST all common sense, and yet we do it anyway. When it comes to business development, all too frequently we ignore our business "friends" in favor of seemingly more desirable (yet unknown) strangers. Our assumption is that somewhere "out there" lies a rainbow of the best prospects, the highest profits, the healthiest possibilities. Despite the fact that most of us have been told that it takes 10 times the effort and expense to capture new customers than it takes to generate new sales from already-established ones, we nonetheless blissfully leap into the chasm of new business development, waving good-bye to our old business friends and treating them as if they never existed.

How else can we explain why publishing an article, as only one example, strikes most folks as a vehicle for getting their message out to a faceless pool of prospects in the larger business universe and then leaning back to see what (if anything) happens? The article comes out, and the author waits and wonders: Will I get any business out of it? Will any readers contact me about my services? Has anyone even seen it?

Meanwhile, the author has forgotten something critical: she has not so much as announced her published article to her current client base and current prospects, much less offered it for review! The very people who know you best or are getting to know you, who already place great stock in who you are and what you offer, who have already plunked money down for your services in the past—these chums get dissed without so much as a fair warning.

If you really want to make your thoughtleading efforts pay off, you must supplement them with reaching out to your "client community." This means clients and customers, past and present, but also prospects, network contacts, colleagues, coworkers, and even vendors. Your most seemingly insignificant business connections should be on this list and should be continually alerted to your thoughtleading victories because of the oldest business adage in the book: you just never know.

Think about it. Your current customers, contacts, and "business friends" are the ones who will truly be interested in your newly published article or book, or your upcoming talk, or your new business service or product. They actually care about the things you do; they actually feel that they have a stake in your business success. Your job is to help them remember this, to keep reminding them, and to educate them constantly about how you can help them again, or how you can help someone they know. Some people refer to this as "top-of-mind" marketing. I call it smart thoughtleading.

Stop Treating Your Customers as Strangers!

Here's how Michael Katz, now president and chief penguin of Blue Penguin Development, specialists in the development of electronic newsletters, came to grips with this revelation at a previous job:

Early one morning in November of 1998, I was sitting in my office putting together my department's budget for the coming year. At the time I was working for a national cable company as director of marketing for its high-speed Internet service. I was responsible for growing our customer base, and for increasing profitability along the way. As I looked at the plan for the coming year, however, it suddenly dawned on me that I was making a big mistake.

Despite the fact that we already had over one million customers for our cable TV service, and despite the fact that my product was being sold as an add-on to those very same customers, almost all of the tactics that I was using treated our customers as if they were strangers.

About 95 percent of my department's resources—both financial and human—were dedicated to direct mail; TV, radio, and newspaper advertising; telemarketing; online banner ads and sponsorships; and even door-to-door sales. Not one of these tactics did anything to either strengthen or leverage the relationships and history that we already had with our own customers.

So we made some changes. We took active steps to create and benefit from our strong relationships with our customers and potential customers. In the process, we saw some incredible results:

- *Our customer base quadrupled in 18 months, going from 40,000 to 160,000.*
- *Our average acquisition costs were cut in half, dropping from $30 per new customer to less than $15.*
- *Our existing customers were passionately engaged in promoting our service to their friends and family, eventually accounting for almost 10 percent of all new sales.*
- *We were able to make faster, more informed decisions about how to run our business, thanks to the constant input that our customers gave us.*
- *Selling and servicing our customers became easier and a lot more enjoyable.*

In short, what we learned was that stronger relationships lead to more profits, faster.

Generating Your Client Community

Let's begin by dissecting the term *client community*. The focus of any successful business is on making clients happy and retaining them forever, as well as on continuing to add new clients and working hard to make them happy too. To achieve the first part, you need good employees, partners, and vendors to help you get the job done right. To achieve the second part, you need a constant stream of prospective clients, as well as influencers (those who spread good word of mouth about you to prospects) and references (those who will attest to your greatness) to drive them your way. So while your client community is all about clients, it also includes many people who are not actually clients at all.

Keeping this image of a client community in mind will redirect your business development efforts in a much more effective direction. Whatever thoughtleading actions you undertake, you'll soon instinctively remember to build in your client community. You'll stop forgetting to alert your client community to your latest published article, speaking engagement, book, media exposure, blog, new product or service, case study, new client, client project, personal insight, or wild idea. You'll stop assuming that 90 percent of your best prospects are out there somewhere in the business galaxy rather than right here on your business home planet. As a result, you'll watch your thoughtleading actions yield concrete results and your business development climb steadily uphill.

In support of this, you must construct an electronic water cooler. This will provide the means for you to get out the latest word about you and to keep it circulating out there, near and far. There'll be no water in the cooler, however—only e-mail addresses. You will use this e-list, composed of all the members of your client community, to educate and reeducate everybody about the value that you offer. The result for you will be a word-of-mouth promotion machine that was unavailable to 99 percent of us back in the ancient pre-Internet days.

How It Works

About five years ago, I began to e-mail my "thoughtnotes" e-letter on a monthly schedule, as opposed to the random e-mailings that I had been doing up to then. I had at least understood the basic principle of the client community, i.e., that unless I let my clients, prospects, colleagues, and others know about the various good work I was doing, the chances that they would find out about it at all were slim. But the next principle I had to understand was the critical difference that regularity can make. I had heard that research showed that this produced results, so I dedicated myself to getting my e-letter out every 30 or so days.

At first, I noticed nothing unusual. After about three months, however, the number of prospects that came my way as a result of referrals seemed to be on the increase. When I asked the standard question, "Where did you hear about me?" the answer tended to be, "So-and-So told me about you." Good old So-and-So invariably was someone on my e-list—a client sometimes, a colleague sometimes, even a prospect sometimes! Receiving my thoughtnotes on a regular basis kept reminding them of what I was doing, and also of the fact that I was still out there doing it.

By six months, I could always count on having half a dozen or so qualified prospects in my pipeline at any one time. Every week brought in new inquiries; some days even brought in half a dozen prospects. Today, some years later, I am never at a loss for qualified prospects. I am never at a point where I wonder where the next client, prospect, project, or meal is coming from. Most times it's all I can do to keep up with what I have on my plate.

Mary Adams and her Trek Consulting cofounder, Michael Oleksak, know exactly what I'm talking about. Mary and Mike have been churning out their own monthly e-newsletter, "Trekking," for years now, and they proudly boast that they have never missed even one month! So what business development results have they reaped from all this go-the-extra-mile effort?

"We regularly get calls from people we know casually or haven't seen in a long time," Adams says.

> They may not be on our minds, but we are on theirs. And so they know to call us or they tell people to call us whenever they see a situation that fits our firm's personality. They don't have to remember an elevator pitch that we did months or years ago; they don't lose their recollection of what we're all about. Our newsletter keeps reminding them! They end up with a deep understanding of our value proposition thanks to the ideas and articles we put forth in our e-newsletter.

Oleksak adds

> But you've got to do it regularly. Research shows that you'll get a better "open rate" if your message arrives at the same time on the same day. And keep "feeding" your e-list.

Also, having a newsletter actually has motivated us to be better networkers. We no longer treat the meeting of someone at a cocktail party as a chance encounter. Once we ask if they would like to receive our newsletter, which they usually agree to, we have then entered into a long-term relationship with them, without which what's the point of networking at all?

It should also be noted that sending e-mails using a software program or Web-based system will also allow you to be "granular," customizing your e-list so that you can send specific messages to particular subgroups. A law firm, for example, can allow its clients to receive communications about new laws or court decisions geared to their specialized interests. An IP law firm could send separate e-mails to those clients most interested in trademarks, or to those clients most interested in patents, or to those clients most interested in international rules changes, and so on. Everyone can be included in an umbrella e-list too, so that messages that are of interest to everyone can be e-mailed en masse.

You Might as Well Throw Away the Card

When I speak before groups on the subject of thoughtleading, I often ask for a show of hands of those who have in fact set up an e-list. Usually, almost everyone in the room raises their hands.

Next I ask for a show of hands from those who actually *use* their e-list, at least sending out a message of some kind here and there, even if as little as once a year. Most, but not all, of those who had raised their hands previously are able to raise their hands once again.

Then I ask for a show of hands from those who send out e-messages on at least a quarterly basis. Many hands stay down this time, although typically about half the room might still be in the game.

Now things start getting rough: "How about a show of hands of those who send out messages to their e-list at least every other month?" There are way fewer hands this time.

Finally I ask the money question: "Who sends out messages to their e-list monthly?" This time, if I see 5 hands rise in a roomful of 100, we're doing pretty good!

Again, if you're not reminding your business friends of what you do and that you're still out there doing it on a very regular basis, you might as well stop wasting your time and energy on business development. When you leave a networking event, just throw all those cards that you picked up into the trash. They're not going to do you any good anyway.

Seriously, though, networking without follow-up, and then without continued follow-up in the form of regular reminders, is opportunity unrealized. Make a commitment to keeping your client community informed and reminded of what's going on with you and your business. Stop assuming that they know this already and that your efforts are better spent targeting complete strangers who could care less.

Putting New People on Your E-list

You can see by now that when I speak of e-lists, I'm not suggesting that you purchase an e-list or borrow someone else's. You really have to build an e-list of your own, culled from your day-to-day meetings and introductions. You also have to follow a few simple rules of e-etiquette, so that you show your client community mutual respect:

- *Tell your new contacts that you'd like to put them on your e-list.* You can do this in person or you can send them an e-mail after you meet them, but do let them know so that they can give you their permission; 95 percent will say, "Thanks."
- *Remind your new contacts they can always unsubscribe, adding that you won't be offended if they do.* Although we all realize that unsubscribing is indeed a standard option, it helps to know that the e-list owner will not take offense if the option is used. This builds trust and may even make your new contact more willing to say yes to receiving your e-mails.

THOUGHT NOTES

Why Very Few People Actually "Unsubscribe"

A colleague of mine named Rudy once told me, "I get a lot of e-mail, and so I don't always have time to read yours. But I'm afraid to unsubscribe, because if I do, I might miss something!"

Why is this advantageous to me? Because as long as Rudy stays on my e-list, even if he never actually reads what I send him, my e-mails keep reminding him that I am still around creating thoughtleaders.

- *Assure your new contacts that you do not send advertisements.* You will be sending your e-letter, your e-tips, announcements of a published book or article, and other types of "e-blasts." You will be sending information that your community can use, including links to Web sites and other services, commentaries in your blog, and links to helpful articles. You will *not* be sending hard-sell solicitations or advertisements. Your new contact will breathe a sigh of relief upon hearing this. Your job is to make sure that you keep your word. Note, however, that there is one exception to this rule: If your business is centered around a product or specialized service (such as floral arrangement, piano tuning, or express delivery), those on your e-list will in fact appreciate receiving direct information about how your product or service works, including (and perhaps especially) notices of discounts, sales, bonus items, and product applications.
- *Inform your new contacts that you do not share your e-mail list with other list makers.* Again, an audible sigh of relief from your new contact will immediately follow this news. Keep your word on this one, too.

- *Tell your new contacts that you'd like to be placed on their e-list as well.* This one is typically forgotten, but what's good for the goose is good for the old gander, right? Networking should not be a one-way street, and besides, being on other folks' lists could help you out as well. If we truly believe in the power of networking, we should want to keep getting reminders from those we met months (or years) ago just as much as we want to keep sending them reminders about us.

Plus, asking to be placed on their e-lists as well suggests that they indeed have an e-list just like you do, or at least that they *should* have. This makes the concept of placing your new contact on your e-list sound like standard operating procedure (which I personally believe it should be) rather than an aberration. One format for asking someone's permission to put him or her on your e-list could thus sound like this: "Let's put each other on our respective e-lists so that we can stay in touch."

Sample Follow-up E-mail Message

Following a networking event, but immediately before you put a new contact onto your e-list, always send that contact a personalized e-mail. This does not have to be long and drawn-out; it's simply a device for continuing this budding relationship and asking the contact for permission to put him or her on your e-list. Without this, all hope of developing your new business friendship is lost.

As an added bonus, your follow-up e-mail offers the opportunity to reinforce your thoughtleading brand, perhaps by sharing one of your published articles. Your new contact will much appreciate this and will say so.

Hello Jim,

It was great to meet you today at the Business Roundtable breakfast. I enjoyed our chat, and I hope we will see each other at a future BR event and do it again. Meanwhile, let's put each other on our respective e-lists and stay in touch.

    I also wanted to share with you one of my recently published articles, "The Essentials of Managing a Team." This article will give you a better understanding of what my company does and how we go about doing it. Click here to see it on my Web site, www.managingnateam.com.

    Thanks again, Jim . . . see you soon!

Regards,

Bill

Notice that e-mail messages work well when they are informal, especially in a case where you have already met the recipient. Notice also the line about putting each other on their respective e-lists. Furthermore, notice that a subtle reminder of Bill's specialty is embedded in the reference to his article, as well as a soft credibility boost by including the words "recently published." Finally, by including a link to his Web site to allow Jim to view the article, he has driven new traffic to his site, creating the possibility that Jim will visit other pages on Bill's site as well.

    In one short but sweet boilerplate e-mail, Bill has unleashed a quadruple business development broadside that does not threaten his new contact, but instead entices him.

Not Necessarily a Newsletter

Here's a response I sometimes hear when I ask members of an audience why they do *not* send out regular e-mails: "Ken, doing an e-newsletter takes a lot of time. I just can't afford it right now." Many folks let this stop them in their tracks.

An e-blast, however, a better term for what we're discussing here, doesn't have to be a full-fledged newsletter. It can be any kind of format you like.

For some people, like Mary Adams and Mike Oleksak at Trek Consulting, putting out a full-scale newsletter works. For others, even the shortest of announcements or tips can do the job. Bill's follow-up e-mail could easily be customized into a terse e-blast basically announcing his article and nothing more.

In between, a format with, say, three or four bullet points might work. Here's a typical e-letter from employee benefits thoughtleader Dan Cassidy. Notice how much he has done in very little space:

New Client

We would like to welcome our newest client, the Brattle Group. The Brattle Group provides consulting services and expert testimony on economic, finance, regulatory, and strategic issues to corporations, law firms, and public agencies worldwide.

You can get more information at its Web site: http://www.brattle.com.

Society of Actuaries

Dan has been appointed the General Officer–Education for the entire Society of Actuaries (SoA). In this role, Dan will be responsible for the course of study of future actuaries primarily in the United States and Canada.

Dan was selected a "Dynamic Leader" by the SoA. The SoA, looking to revitalize its brand image, chose about a dozen actuaries who are leading the industry forward. This was a great honor for Dan—and very much fun—he was filmed on location at Walden Pond in Concord, MA. Watch out, Hollywood!

Published Articles

The article "Megatrends in Retirement Planning" by Dan Cassidy appeared in *Employment Relations Today,* published by Wiley InterScience. To read the article, please click here.

Recent Presentations

Dan spoke at a recent NEEBC conference on 401(k) fees— "Do you know where your participants' money goes?" If you would like a copy of the presentation, please e-mail Audrey Anthony at Audrey@cassidyretirement.com.

NEHRA

Dan will speak at the upcoming NEHRA 2007 Benefits Seminar, "Changing Concepts, New Legislation and the Challenges of Communication," to be held on January 26, 2007, at the Westin Hotel in Waltham, MA.

Topics of discussion will be the results of the 2006 Employee Benefits Trends Survey conducted by Aon Consulting, which polled over 1,000 employers on trends in retirement, health-care, and benefit communications.

Click on the link to find out more information about this seminar: http://www.nehra.com/events/eventdetail.cfm?id=221.

See how Dan managed to squeeze his recent thoughtleading actions into small spaces? His article title alone communicates his expertise in the area of retirement planning, and his two speaking titles promote other aspects of his expertise. In addition, by listing both a presentation he has just completed and one that is coming up, he communicates that public speaking is something that he does on an ongoing basis, reminding his client community that he is available for speaking to groups that they are involved with as well.

How long does it take for Dan to compose such an e-blast? About half a day, he admits. Yet the branding impact that this yields in return may be too high to measure.

The key, then, to communicating with your client community is not so much that you've got to publish a regular voluminous newsletter, but rather that you need to find a way to systematize your communications so that you won't be able to dredge up the excuse that you just don't have time.

Find a way to make this work and the benefits will be obvious and enormous. Let your assumptions about how much time this has to take keep holding you back and something else will be sure to occur: you'll be forgotten.

Publishing Online: The Better Way to Go?

Opportunities to be published online now abound and are expanding exponentially. There are so many Web sites looking for articles to keep them fresh, so many e-newsletters seeking articles, so many online versions of print publications looking for articles—the e-landscape is wide open.

And if you wonder whether online publications may be less effective or less credible than those published in the traditional hard-copy format, then it's time to get yourself out of the Dark Ages. For many reasons, online publication is now the way to go.

Beyond the issue of credibility, which I'll address later, publishing online has many advantages over print—so many, in fact, that I would venture to deem it vastly superior. For example:

- Publishing online allows your article (and you, your bio, and your firm) to show up on Google.
- Publishing online allows easy forwarding of your article to your own contacts and your e-list.
- Publishing online allows your readers to locate your article easily on your Web site.
- Publishing online allows your readers to send you an immediate reaction via e-mail.
- If there is a typo or other error, publishing online permits quick and simple corrections to be made, even well after publication.

- Publishing online permits your article to be quickly and easily updated whenever you wish, even well after publication.

In defense of traditional hard-copy publication, what can you say in rebuttal? That a hard-copy publication is shiny and fits snugly in your hands? Well, yes, sometimes—but not always!

In terms of the credibility factor, while it's true that many hard-copy offline publications will surely garner a certain level of desirability because of their high name recognition (Harvard Business Review, the *Wall Street Journal*, and *CFO* magazine come to mind immediately), to be able to brag that you were published in *Strategic Finance* magazine (a hard-copy publication) rather than *Finance Executive Online* tends not to earn you all that many extra points. How about *Chief Executive* magazine versus its online version, Chiefexecutive.net? How about Industryweek.com vs. the floppy *Industry Week* print edition? Given that the online versions are infinitely easier to get into than the extremely space-challenged offline versions, is it really worth all that much more time and trouble to set your sights on print rather than online? If you say yes, you're either someone with a lot of time on your hands or a dreamer who isn't likely to wage this long, tough battle in the first place.

In addition to the items on the previous bulleted list, publishing online means that your article will be archived and thus be available for viewing indefinitely. With print publishing, your article will last a month at best, then get relegated to the trash or the library stacks, where oxygenation will one day do it in.

THOUGHT NOTES

Google Loves Links

One less tangible result of publishing articles on the Web, though an effect that is more tangible than I would have thought, is that Google and other search engines place

> heavy emphasis on sites that link back to your own site. As a
> result, I've found that having articles published all over the
> place, including your company's Web site or your e-mail
> link positioned in your bio, tremendously increases your
> Internet visibility and especially Google search rankings.
>
> —Curtis Bingham, president,
> Predictive Consulting Group

And getting published online still distinguishes you from those who have never been published. You wrote an article, and an unbiased editor reviewed it and made the decision to publish it, i.e., share it with her readers. Online or offline, this does not happen unless someone in a position of editorial authority deems your article and ideas a worthwhile, significant contribution.

There is a seeming downside, however. Publishing online exposes your article to the risk of piracy. This means that you may very well find that your article has been published on other Web sites without your permission. And there is no practical way to stop this. Copying and pasting has become such a rampant practice nowadays that you'd need to spend all your waking time fighting it in order to make even the smallest dent.

But is this actually a problem? If we recall why we write articles for publication in the first place, it is to get our name and our ideas spread around. The good thing about these pirates is that, although they are lifting our articles without our permission, they are also leaving our names and bios (and sometimes our photos) intact so that we are still getting the appropriate credit in addition to expanding our promotional bandwidth. So today's article "pirates" in fact do us a great service, vigorously expanding our visibility without asking us to lift a finger. They are out there working for us, they're not charging us for their actions that promote us, and they're staying out of our face. In helping themselves to our goods, they increase the chances that our goods will deliver us fruit.

A lengthier version of my article on thoughtleading, for example, was published initially in a major business journal called the *Handbook of Business Strategy.* I then placed this article on my Web site—and the fun began! In the three years since, hundreds upon hundreds of Web sites have plugged it in, none of them having asked my permission. Yet the result has been a bonanza of Google hits. If you Google my name or the word "thoughtleading," you'll reap links to my article on over 20 pages. And they keep showing up by the dozens with each passing week.

To Blog or Not to Blog

What about blogs? Are they a good idea? Are they in synch with the thoughtleading approach? Are they worth your time and trouble?

Like other thoughtleading actions, a blog will powerfully set you apart if you treat it as a tool. Simply posting a blog entry every day or so, then passively hoping that someone will see it will not help you. Remember that for thoughtleading to be effective, it must be treated as a verb. So find ways to proactively promote your blog and draw readers your way, rather than waiting for them to come. "If you build it, they will come" does not apply here.

Use your e-blasts to promote your blog and to announce your latest entries. Set up a special e-list just for your blog subscribers, but don't neglect to include them in your umbrella e-blasts as well. You want, after all, to keep your blog readers as informed as anyone else about your services and expertise. It probably helps both you and them only minimally if all they receive from you are blog musings and meanderings.

Should you decide to set up a blog, heed these tips for making this thoughtleading tool a success:

1. *Blog frequently, to keep your blog vital.* Otherwise visitors will stop coming, tired of not finding anything new there.
2. *Keep blog entries short.* If your blog entries are very long, your visitors will resist coming back, feeling that reading your blog entries takes too much time. Word of mouth will spread, but that will work against you. New visitors will stay away, not being willing to even try out your blog.

3. *Blog as a firm.* To prevent burnout, employ your entire firm to produce your blog. This way, no one partner, associate, manager, or staffer is fully responsible for all the postings. This distributes the workload, keeping blog entries fresh and varied and involving your whole firm in positioning its thoughtleading ideas.

Web Sites for Thoughtleaders

From a thoughtleading point of view, your Web site should emphasize precisely this: you and your firm are the leading experts and thinkers in your profession. This dictates some seemingly obvious Web site sections that on the majority of business Web sites, astonishingly, are nowhere to be found. I'm talking about such sections as "Published Articles," "Published Books," "Speaking Engagements," "Media and News," and "Surveys and Research." Naturally, an e-mail sign-up box will be readily visible as well, the better to grow your client community list. An archive of your past e-blasts is a must.

Most Web sites will contain only standard sections like "About Us," "Our Services," "Our Client List," and "Contact Us." You should have these sections too, but if that's all you've got, you'll look and feel (and be) just like everybody else. The thoughtleading sections allow you to highlight the extra lengths you go to in order to be the top expert out there, the go-to authority that people turn to, or should turn to, every time.

For example, in your speaking section, highlight your Speaking Topics List and your Target Audience List, niftily advertising your speaking services in the process. Include your speaking engagement calendar too: where and when you will be speaking next, and on what topics. Link such listings to your event sponsor's Web site so that your own visitors can easily learn more as well as register. Keep all your past engagements posted so that soon you'll have an impressive record of your speaking prowess right there for all eyes to see. Also in your speaking section, post your speaker sheet. This gives meeting planners the chance to glimpse your credentials and review your glowing testimonials.

Similarly, post articles in both PDF and text form so that your PDF reprints will truly impress your visitors, while the text version can be picked up by search engines (PDFs can't be). You'll be eternally grateful for this advice one day when you are late for a speaking engagement or sales call and you need to grab some article handouts but fast! It'll then be simple and quick to click over to your Web site article section, print out a few color copies, then burst out of your office for your meeting. Believe me, this works great when you need it to—I know!

If you have reached the thoughtleading pantheon, meaning that you are the author of a book, your book cover must be highlighted on your home page with a link to more information on a special book page inside. You might also post another link to Amazon, BN.com, or another Web site where your visitors can purchase your book, as well as to testimonials of your book, perhaps a sample page or two, your book's table of contents, and other such information. The key here is not to forget that a book is your absolute best thoughtleading expert's calling card, packing a credibility wallop via a third-party endorsement (your publisher's) that cannot be beat. If you have a book, or as soon as you publish one, do not forget to revamp your Web site in such a way that your visitors cannot escape knowing about it.

12

Pillar 5: Making Vigorous Use of the Media

That's it, baby! When you got it, flaunt it! Flaunt it!

MEL BROOKS

WITH PILLAR 5, making use of the media, we finally reach the spot at which most individuals, companies, and even public relations (PR) and publicity departments and firms typically begin—and end! You might write a press release announcing newly hired personnel or a new product or service or the opening of a new store or branch office or the promotion of an inside middle manager to a new executive position. If you get really risqué, you might comment on an industry trend or some recent news event.

You'll then distribute your press release to mainstream newspapers, business magazines, the industry trade press, and/or professional journals. If you currently employ even a large public relations firm to perform for you what I call "traditional PR," you may notice that even with your sizable monthly retainer, a plethora of press releases and the occasional interview with a business publication is pretty much all you get.

Beyond such traditional PR, there's not much else going on. Have you ever been interviewed by a radio reporter or invited to be a guest on a TV talk show? These too are traditional PR (TPR) activities, although unless you're involved in something very hot, they'll likely be few and far between. Sometimes your TPR will get you a nice profile of you and your business in a publication, although these too will be few and far between. Also, once you get such a profile, you can say good-bye to any further major publicity in that publication for a long time to come. The publication will not want its readers to get the impression that its business coverage is repeating itself.

Why don't TPR firms also provide thoughtleading services? Truthfully, many of them don't really know how to go about it. Developing articles for publications may come closest to being an action that they are familiar with, but their usual approach here is to ghostwrite the articles for their clients, which ends up taking more time than anyone would like, and thus the process bogs down in frustration and in the missing of deadlines. An AIL, for example, is a tool that few TPR specialists have ever considered (or imagined).

Books? Forget it! Most TPR practitioners have zero experience with the book-publishing industry. Almost none of them have ever written a book themselves, and few of them have the slightest clue about how to serve as a literary agent. Given that book publishing is fraught with twists and turns born of its own peccadilloes (book proposals, agents' percentages, arcane contract clauses, and so on), the learning curve can be extremely steep. It becomes far easier to avoid such bewildering details altogether and just keep pumping out endless press releases.

Speaking engagements offer a similar potential quicksand. Setting up speaking gigs, helping with speeches, coaching the speaker client, negotiating with meeting planners, comforting the speaker client after a disappointing performance or low turnout: these again are skill sets that most TPR experts simply do not possess—or want to. It's better to keep speaking-as-a-strategy tucked safely away on a quickly forgotten back burner.

Employing TPR at all in the service of thoughtleading, therefore, requires upending its conventional emphasis. Yes, I do recommend sending out press releases, but not mindlessly and not just about mundane news. Yes, try to get reporters to interview you, but see this as an adjunct to your published articles and books, not as the whole ball of wax. Yes, find ways to generate publicity for yourself and your firm, including radio and TV and Internet appearances, but see these as opportunities to promote your latest book or article or speaking engagement. Because in and of themselves, these TPR activities will not make you, but they could very well break you.

Whatever forms of traditional PR you engage in, the results will frequently fit into a boom-or-bust scenario. Publicity in the form of being briefly quoted, for example, or being mentioned inside a larger article or by a featured columnist, or even having an article devoted entirely to a profile of your firm and its services, often produces—nothing! You may even find yourself hard-pressed to locate or encounter anyone in your world who has even seen it.

On the other hand, the total opposite can occur, with either positive or negative repercussions. You might be misquoted, for example, or have a comment taken out of context in such a way that you (1) sound as though you don't know what you're talking about, (2) alienate someone—colleagues, customers, the general public, or even friends and family—or (3) appear to say something very different from your original intention.

Back during the presidential campaign of 1968, for example, Michigan Governor George Romney (Mitt Romney's dad) was asked about his impressions of the Vietnam War just after returning from a fact-finding mission there. Romney used the words "I was brainwashed" to describe the deception practiced by the U.S. military and the Johnson administration in their public pronouncements on how the war was going. Out of context, however, this phrase was quickly taken to mean that Romney had a weak character and was easily deceived, despite the fact that everyone who knew him saw him as a talented, sharp, decisive thinker. Those three words proved the undoing of his presidential hopes.

Positive Explosion

On the boom side of what TPR can deliver to you, which unfortunately is what far too many believe to be the typical scenario, its execution can produce a veritable positive explosion. An article can be written about your firm or a quote of yours can appear that, for whatever reason, touches off a desirable bombshell, sending inquiring business prospects crashing your way, many of them presold to buy whatever it is you're selling.

This actually happened in the early days of an earlier business of mine called CareerScape when, without thinking much about it, Barbara (my partner) and I added editors, reporters, columnists, and TV/radio contacts to our snail-mail list, then began sending them not only press releases, but our quarterly newsletters and promotional postcards as well. One columnist who began receiving these was Juliet F. Brudney, the author of a very popular *Boston Globe* weekly column about careers and jobs, a column that she had by that time been penning for many years.

Somewhat unnerved by the fact that she had never heard of our CareerScape company, she called us up to check us out. "So, are you making a living at this?" she asked suspiciously. We assured her that we were. "Well, how are you different?" For the next half hour we shared with her the various creativity and self-focus techniques that we had integrated into our career development process, including the addition of play-oriented exercises and an emphasis on meaning and passion.

Juliet followed up her interview with us by interviewing five graduates of our program, then set to work writing what came to be an entire column about our unique program. When the column came out two weeks later, its headline read as if some high-priced ad agency had composed it for a major advertising campaign.

"Looking for a Dream Job? Now There's a Way to Get One!" went the headline. Juliet's column then went on to report glowingly on many positive differences between our CareerScape approach and conventional career programs, as well as results and testimonials from our satisfied customers.

I picked up my *Globe* at 7:45 a.m. that Tuesday morning and was excited about how we were being treated, but then I wondered what, if anything, might come of it. By 8 a.m., I found out as first one phone call, then a second, then a third, then a fourth came in—within the first 15 minutes!

By 9 a.m., the phone was ringing off the proverbial hook; the circuits were overloading, and busy signals were frustrating callers who could not get through. They even began calling Juliet to ask why the phone number she had published didn't work!

That day alone, about 100 calls got through, and the next day even more, and the next day more still. For weeks after, the phone kept this up, ringing so much that by the time things finally began calming down, our business, though only a year old, had grown a hundredfold. Our programs and coaching slots were now booked weeks in advance, and inquiries, though not at the intense level of those explosive first weeks, continued to come in steadily.

This kind of astonishing result from TPR can happen, but it is a mistake to believe that it is typical or probable. Why did this happen to us? What did we do to make it happen? Is there a formula you can adhere to so as to replicate it?

One can speculate about such things, but one can never really know: Was it because Juliet's column had such a glowing, right-on-the-money headline? Was it because her column was a particularly popular one, read by exactly our target market? Was it because her own longtime popularity all by itself drove her loyal readers to call us? Was it because she had somehow written the perfect description of what we were doing in such a way that it touched all the right readers' buttons?

All of these are potential factors, but heeding and replicating them does not ensure a similar reaction. In fact, one year later, Juliet wrote a similar article about us (albeit shorter and thus not so detailed), and while inquiries again came in, there were far fewer of them, and they did not all come at once. Around the same time, when another excellent profile of our services appeared in the same *Boston Globe*, this time written by a staff reporter (not by Juliet), only three phone calls resulted. We made many attempts to replicate the Juliet explosion, including getting ourselves on TV and even in her column on the average of once per year, yet none of these subsequent TPR victories came close.

The important lesson is that, although a massive positive customer reaction *can* happen, it probably won't. When engaging in TPR, then, don't lose that perspective.

Tying TPR to Thoughtleading

But if all too often absolutely nothing happens, or next to nothing, one would be justified in asking: Why bother at all? Why not just write articles and books, do fresh research, deliver talks and presentations, and leverage the Internet? Why not forget publicity, media attention, and TPR altogether?

The reason to tie TPR to your other thoughtleading actions is what I call the "nudge factor." With so much going on in our daily lives—the bombardment of advertising, e-mail come-ons, junk mail, digital billboards in elevators, TV commercials, movie trailers, Internet pop-ups, and on and on and on—you've got draw upon as many ways as you can to cut through all this noise. Little things here and there will nudge your other thoughtleading actions along, nudging along awareness of you and your firm in small bites, nudging those into coalitions with larger bites, nudging your target market in your direction, nudging this here, nudging that there, nudging until . . . bang! Your name and your business are imprinted in a tipping point of more and more of your prospects' minds.

"Oh, yeah, I've heard about you," you suddenly encounter someone saying. "You're an XYZ expert, right?"

To which you, the now somewhat famous XYZ expert, respond, "Yes, that's right. How did you hear of me?"

Your nudged prospect now replies, "I don't know exactly. I've been hearing about you for a while now. From all over, really."

When this starts happening, your nudge factor is hard at work as prospects and other contacts begin awakening to your existence as an XYZ expert on a level that affords you high credibility—even if those who have heard of you can't seem to place how or even why they have heard of you. It matters that they have heard at all! By default you become the go-to authority on XYZ—bar none.

One key to ensuring that the nudge factor works wonders for you is to attach TPR to your thoughtleading strategy as a supplement to the other four pillars, not as the primary game in town. To reap the potential benefits of this, you'll need to employ this pillar continuously, hammering away at getting the good word out about your other thoughtleading actions via TPR channels, thus nudging your client community toward the top-of-mind certainty that you, and you alone, are the thoughtleader to turn to every time.

Thoughtleading Press Releases

There are tiny things that you can do to ensure that your use of TPR will always be tied to your thoughtleading actions. They are small and at first glance of seemingly low importance, but when you really consider them, the strength of their use becomes more apparent. By employing them, you keep all your thoughtleading efforts coordinated and working to the max.

To begin with, make the core of your press releases some kind of news of a thoughtleading action, such as a recently published article, a speaking gig, or the results of a survey. Don't waste a lot of time with announcements of new personnel, new clients captured, celebration of your firm's fifth or seventy-fifth anniversary, or whatever. I'm not saying that you can't or shouldn't send out such press releases; I'm just reiterating that if such content represents your most common press release strategy, you're missing the opportunity to use TPR to bolster your other four thoughtleading pillars.

What might potential thoughtleading-based press releases look like? Here are a few good examples:

1. *Announcement of a just-published article.* "Formidable Company is pleased to announce that an article 'How to Keep Your Revenues High' by its CEO, M. J. Helper, has just been published in *Business Wisdom Journal*. Ms. Helper's article details innovative business development and customer retention strategies. In it, Ms. Helper suggests that 'companies that match their business development efforts with customer satisfaction tactics will invariably find themselves at the top of their industry's list of highest revenue producers.' If you wish to read the full article, click here: LINK (to Formidable Web site).

   Variation: announcement of the acceptance of an article to be published at a later date. You can quote from the article the same way and even post a preview version of it on your Web site so that readers of your releases can click on your site to read it in advance of its actual publication.

2. *Announcement of a just-published book.* "Formidable Company is pleased to announce the publication of a new book by its CEO, M. J. Helper, *How to Keep Your Revenues High*, published by Good Biz Publishers. Ms. Helper's book details innovative business development and customer retention strategies, suggesting that 'companies that match their business development efforts with customer satisfaction tactics will invariably find themselves at the top of their industry's list of highest revenue producers.' For info on how to purchase a copy of *How to Keep Your Revenues High*, click here: LINK (to Formidable Web site).

   Variation: announcement of signing a contract with a publisher for a book to be published at a later date. Again, you can announce your book in advance and include quotes from you the author on the planned content of your book, as well as how it will be a useful book for your target market to read.

3. *Announcement of an upcoming speaking engagement and its topic.* "Formidable Company is pleased to announce that its CEO, M. J. Helper, has been invited to speak to the City

Business Forum on the topic 'How to Keep Your Revenues High' on Friday, June 10, 2008. Ms. Helper's talk will detail innovative business development and customer retention strategies. During her presentation, Ms. Helper will suggest that 'companies that match their business development efforts with customer satisfaction tactics will invariably find themselves at the top of their industry's list of highest revenue producers.' If you wish to learn more about this upcoming presentation, click here: LINK (to Formidable Web site or to City Business Forum site).

Variation: announcement of a recent speaking engagement and topic. My own bias, however, favors announcing your speaking engagements in advance whenever possible so that you can help promote the event and possibly draw a larger crowd.

4. *Announcement of a just-completed survey.* "Formidable Company is pleased to announce the completion of its recent survey of 250 CFOs of Fortune 500 companies on the topic 'How to Keep Your Revenues High.' Formidable CEO M. J. Helper reports that the survey results clearly demonstrate that 'companies that match their business development efforts with customer satisfaction tactics invariably find themselves at the top of their industry's list of highest revenue producers.' If you wish to learn more about this valuable survey and how to obtain a copy, click here: LINK (to Formidable Web site).

Variation: announcement based on one piece of the survey. Research produces a wealth of information that cannot always be adequately summarized in a single press release. So why not mine your survey for multiple press releases, thus extending the mileage from your survey's content and keeping your thoughtleading actions up and running throughout an entire year?

Do you get the picture here? Notice how the very same topic can be utilized in a variety of ways. Your core message becomes a thread running through all your thoughtleading actions. Press releases can then be distributed announcing every one of them.

When the Media Call, Respond at Once!

When a reporter responds to your press release, don't treat him or her as just another call to return after you've gotten through your other calls, even if the others came in well before the reporter's. To the extent you can, drop everything that's on your plate and return the media call right away. To really make friends with the media and to get them to keep calling you again and again, respect their need to make their often tight deadlines and do what you can to spend as much time with them as they need, and as soon as they need it.

Granted, sometimes this won't be possible, as you'll be jammed up with your own deadlines or in the middle of a critical meeting with a client or prospect. But reporters live and die by their deadlines, so those who find a way to consistently accommodate them on a moment's notice will be first in line to be called for a quote on a breaking news story.

My brother Ed, a financial planner with Ameriprise Financial in Braintree, Massachusetts, paid attention to my advice on this when a *Boston Globe* reporter called him out of the blue to get his comment on a financial topic that had just broken in the news. Ed was so knowledgeable and helpful to the reporter that only two weeks later this same reporter, now working on a different article, called Ed again. Within one month, Ed got quoted in two major news articles in one of the country's leading daily newspapers.

Dan Cassidy, the retirement benefits planning thoughtleader and author of *A Manager's Guide to Strategic Retirement Plan Management*, also took this same advice when a reporter from Wall Street Journal Radio responded to one of his press releases. Because Dan spent a few minutes with this reporter at a moment's notice, and because he also made himself available when the same reporter called a few weeks later, Dan ended up getting his ideas aired on Wall Street Journal Radio multiple times over the next few years.

On the flip side, reports my "PR Czar" Henry Stimpson, founder and principal of Stimpson Communications, an experienced TPR specialist, there was a time early in his career when, as a reporter for a financial services publication, he received a callback one day from a potential interviewee that he had tried to reach four months before!

"I actually thought that was pretty funny," he recalls now. "My deadline that day had been four hours from the time of my call. Getting back to me four *months* later was a bit ineffective."

Best Practices for Winning Media Attention

In addition to stopping whatever else you're doing and giving a calling reporter your full attention, there are other best practices for winning and retaining the media's attention to keep in mind. Always attempt, for example, to be as informative, candid, and forthcoming as you possibly can. Don't be concerned, as many folks are, about spilling too much of what you know, i.e., "giving away the store." The media want you to be authentic and informative, not cagey and canned, which will only turn them off and probably win you no space in their article at all.

So help them out genuinely and enthusiastically with all the expert content you can provide. They are neither out to get you nor attempting to steal your secrets. They only want to understand an issue or news development from multiple perspectives so that they can stitch it all together and adequately inform their readers.

Also, if you wish to pitch an article idea to the press, i.e., an article that *they* will write instead of you, you must think up something provocative. The media are not interested in doing an article about you just because you are a good guy or because your clients have told you that you've done them some good. A gazillion professionals can claim that, including every one of your competitors.

Think about what makes you different. Why are you special or unique? What ideas do you come up with that no one else does? What makes you a thoughtleader? Henry Stimpson cites a client of his, Frank

Congemi, a top-rated financial planner, as one example of how to do this well. As Henry recalls:

> *What worked like a charm for Frank, was that he was registered not just as a financial planner but as an RFG: a Registered Financial Gerontologist. The media were quite intrigued by that, as they'd never heard of such a thing. Indeed, there weren't many other RFGs out there at all. This gave me what I needed to get Frank into articles or news reports having to do with elderly retirement. Plus Frank was very outspoken, not afraid to attack financial regulators and accuse them of not doing their jobs. Sometimes I even had to rein him in, but the overall effect of this unique combination was to make him very attractive to the media.*

Stories quoting or profiling Frank appeared in the *LA Times*, the *NY Daily News*, WNBC-TV, and many more. Sometimes the reporters interviewed his clients as well, all satisfied customers. This represented an advertising bonanza for Frank's business that mere money simply cannot buy.

"His gerontology designation gave him an extra seriousness and scientific credibility that the vast majority of his financial planner competitors didn't possess," Henry explains. "Frank had a designation that was different, which made the media wonder: What is it? What does it mean to you and me? That created a certain allure."

Henry adds

> *Your expertise is your raw material. You have to work with what you have when vying for media exposure, and part of the reason they'll interview you is simply that you raised your hand and let them know you're available. But they're also always on the lookout for something special that makes an individual or firm stand out. Find a way to do that and the media will keep on knocking on your door.*

THOUGHT NOTES

Be Thought-Provoking!

Heath Shackleford writes in his article "Want Press? Become a Thought Leader!" that,

As a true expert, you will bring something new to the party in the way of perspective. In most cases, reporters are not looking for fence sitters; they are looking for someone with a clear point of view, otherwise known as an opinion. This means that you will have to be dramatic in your speech, compelling with your insight and bold with your predictions. Bottom Line: This will require that you take risks from time to time, but if you aren't comfortable with that, you shouldn't be playing the news media game in the first place.

Mistakes to Avoid

We discussed previously the possibility of media attention resulting in a negative development. What should you do, for example, if you should ever find yourself in the unfortunate position of being misquoted? Or maybe an article got some facts wrong about you or your company? What if you were interviewed by a reporter for an hour or more and then when the article appeared, you weren't even in it?

If any of these things should ever happen to you and you find yourself wondering what to do about it, I have three little words for you: let it go. If you want to get yourself quoted and in the media on a regular basis, you've got to understand that these kinds of things happen. They are rarely malicious; they are rarely done on purpose; they're just either a mistake or an unavoidable casualty of media reality. If you didn't end up in an article for which you were interviewed, for example, it was probably because the reporter or editor ran out of space. It happens; let it go. Get over it.

Despite the rampant cynicism in our society today about the press, 99 percent of editors, reporters, and freelance writers are not out to get you. Particularly in the business press, hatchet jobs are not their specialty. Most media people are hard-working professionals like you and me who are intent on doing the best job they possibly can, and with integrity, in a way that serves their readers. When they occasionally get something wrong, it's usually an honest mistake. Period.

Although a misquotation or an inaccurate fact, especially one that casts you or your firm in a bad light, can be understandably upsetting, don't bolt for the phone or your keyboard to take the publication to task. Sit back, calm yourself, and cool off. The hard truth about such episodes is this: there's nothing you can really do about it.

Yes, you can rant and rave and read a reporter the riot act. Yes, you can even insist that the publication print a "correction" in its next issue or that the reporter apologize for the error or infraction. But you need to understand that even if a correction is printed, it will show up in some relatively obscure section of the publication, maybe way at the bottom of page 2 or 3, and in relatively fine print. The plain fact is that, of all the people who even realized that you were misquoted or that a factual error was made, *you* are the only one who will end up seeing the correction because you will be the only one combing the pages for it.

The best advice, instead, is to suck it up, grin and bear it, and then move on. This is the gamble you take when you play with the media. Sometimes your luck pays off, as it did when Juliet Brudney wrote her column in the *Boston Globe* about our CareerScape program. Other times, the resulting article may contain a few blemishes, but you'll be the only one obsessing about it, spending far too much time kvetching and wailing. Basically, if you can't stand the heat of the media game, then get out of their kitchen.

The point is that you just never can know how an article or a TV or radio feature will look before it's put together. And there's nothing at all you can do to direct the final result because it's the media's job to draw conclusions from their interviews and put the whole picture together. They will never consult you. They will never let you see or approve their article or feature, so don't even ask. How you come out in the final analysis is the risk you take for potentially great free publicity. If you want a guarantee, get out your credit card and purchase some advertising.

Even More Mistakes to Avoid

Are there other considerations you should embrace before you decide to add media and TPR to your thoughtleading repertoire? Henry Stimpson has a few thoughts on that subject, in the form of a short piece he has written called "How to Guarantee Your Press Releases Will Be Completely Ignored." We would all do well to heed his hard-earned insights:

- Build your press releases and news hooks entirely around your vanity and ego.
- Brag from start to finish about yourself and your company, i.e., "sell yourself" and avoid offering real information.
- Include lots of buzzwords, peppering your releases and interviews with such phrases as "end-to-end ROI," "scale visionary initiatives," and "drive transparent paradigms." That'll get rid of them!
- Inflate a brief announcement into a massive tome. Make editors work hard to understand what your core message really is.
- Use long, windy quotes in your releases from company insiders that basically have nothing to say. Avoid any and all really meaty substantial information.
- Send out lots of press releases that announce nothing much of importance. The media will soon get the message that your releases deserve a quick click to the recycle icon.
- Use eccentric Capitalization and odd, Punctuation.
- Never bother to proofread or spell-check your releases. Just send 'em out as is, typos be damned.

- Bonus Tip: Apply a similar philosophy to your Web site, brochures, advertisements, articles, e-mail, newsletters, and speaking gigs to make sure everyone will ignore all of those as well.

Gaining free media attention and successfully conducting TPR is not hard. It does, however, require some imagination on your part and the willingness to accommodate the media so that they can fulfill their typically immediate needs. Business media stories come about when reporters and editors get wind of novel or intriguing ideas—that's why they call it "news"—and their sources for such news will most often be experts like you and me. They do want to hear from us, they do want to learn about what we're doing, and they do want to report our success in changing the world. So talk to them, fill them in, help them understand—and don't keep them waiting!

THOUGHT NOTES

More Mistakes to Watch Out For

As if the mistakes shared in this chapter weren't enough, here are three more mistakes that business folks have come up with to ensure that the media stay away:

1. *Corporate censorship.* As companies grow, they become overly protective, instituting guidelines to prevent any company representative from saying the wrong thing or giving away a company secret. Often this translates into censorship, such as in a rule stating that no one should talk to the media without the public relations department being present or approval from upper management. Before long the media start calling the company's more cooperative and responsive competition.

2. *Thinking a relationship with a media representative is all you need.* No matter how well you know an editor or reporter, you still must respond quickly, candidly, and knowledgably to an interviewer's questions. Having a buddy-buddy relationship with a reporter or columnist is good as far as it goes, but in the end it will only get you through the door. After that, ya gotta deliver.

3. *Assuming that off the record means off the record.* When you sit down with a reporter, anything you say can be included in the ultimate story. Don't assume that a reporter will do you any favors in terms of what you'd like put in the story and what you'd like kept out. A reporter is not your friend, at least not at that moment. If you offer something that you absolutely do not want included in a story, the rule is, before you confide your tidbit, say, "This is off the record." You must say this *before* you share your secret, not after.

But even then, you can never be sure that the reporter will honor your request. So my best advice is simple as pie: never say anything "off the record," no matter how tempting or how much you trust your interviewer. You just never can be sure.

13

Maximizing Your Expert's Edge

Sales, Relationships, and a Loyal Following

Thought is the blossom; language the bud; action the fruit behind it.

RALPH WALDO EMERSON

NONE OF THE STEPS we've discussed so far make much difference, of course, if they don't lead to sales. All the article credits, all the hours spent crafting a book, all the speaking engagements that produce positive audience reaction, all the fresh thinking, all the e-blasts to your client community, all the media attention: none of it matters if it doesn't lead to sales.

The reason we engage in thoughtleading or any other business development strategy is to, ahem, develop business. We want thoughtleading to help us build our businesses and keep them strong. We want people to turn to us as the go-to authority every time because that means that our customers are continually coming back to us, and are also sending their friends our way in a steady stream. If thoughtleading has any value, it's the ability to deliver new business on an ongoing basis while maintaining a loyal following of old business. That's the expert's edge.

Yet many beginning thoughtleaders give up on this strategy after a few weeks or a few months out of frustration because writing and publishing three or four articles has failed to produce any results. Speaking engagements, original research, media, Internet visibility: nothing. What the heck's this all about?

The fault, however, my dear thoughtleading Brutus, may not be in the thoughtleading stars but in thyself. Ask yourself these questions:

- How hard have you been working to leverage your thoughtleading actions?
- To what extent have you been leveraging your articles, books, and speaking engagements?
- Do you have your client community e-list in place, and have you been sending out regular e-blasts to the people on your list?
- What about sales? Have you been sharpening your selling skills and tying your marketing and sales efforts directly to your thoughtleading?
- Have you been paying attention to where your prospects are coming from?
- Do you continue to pump out new thoughtleading concepts, or did you stop trying after a couple of published articles, convincing yourself that you'd done enough for now?

No business development strategy can possibly be successful if effective follow-up measures are not consistently practiced and improved. When you walk into that prospect's office, the one that came your way because of a speaking engagement you just did, how do you handle this next step? Do you move the process along skillfully, or do you assume that your prospect is already sold? The truth is, when it comes to selling, you can never be certain that the deal is done until the ink on both your signatures is dry. So while thoughtleading may have done its job of getting you in the door, thoughtleading alone can't save you now. It's time to ramp up good old-fashioned selling procedures.

Do you perceive yourself as a salesperson at all? Many people don't, preferring to just "do the work," and this is frequently their undoing. "Well, I'm just not a salesman," they say. It's an easy out because 99 percent of the people they meet will agree with them and let them off the hook. "I know what you mean," well-meaning colleagues will respond, "I'm not a salesman either."

If this sounds like you, cut it out right now. The truth is that if we are in business, even if we don't own a business or have direct responsibility for sales, we are all sales reps, whether we like it or not. If you own a business, of course, you definitely can't get away from it. Potential customers come your way or you go out in search of them, and when you find them, you must do something about it. Unless your product or service resolves some dire necessity that your customers can't live without, then you've got to sell yourself and your product or service. There's no getting around it.

Take the case of a plumber who gets a frantic call from a homeowner saying that her "toilet is clogged and overflowing; the water is gurgling up right now!" At such a moment, this service provider has no need to sell himself. His prospective customer is begging him to come over.

But if the same plumber receives a call later in the day about replacing a kitchen sink, he may have to behave like a salesman in order to win this business. Perhaps the homeowner has some curiosity about what other sink designs may be available as she considers renovating her kitchen. She is window-shopping right now, but she will make a firm decision soon, so how the plumber treats her will be the deciding factor in whether she hires him or someone else.

If he is pleasant, knowledgeable, flexible, price-sensitive, and accommodating, he may very well win her business. If his demeanor convinces her that he is an expert who can help her sort things out, she may not even ring up anyone else. He will have separated himself from his competition—obliterated it, in fact. He may very well go on to become the go-to plumber she will turn to every time.

However, should the plumber adopt the attitude that he's "not a salesman," he could instead completely blow it. If he acts aloof, bored, annoyed, too busy, or unaware of the latest kitchen sink options (or unwilling to spend time explaining them), the homeowner will pleasantly say good-bye, hang up, and call up another plumber listed in the Yellow Pages. In such a case, simply being a terrific plumber will not suffice.

But what about that feeling that by nature you're simply not a salesperson? Can this be changed? Can selling prowess be learned? Recalling our earlier discussion about whether thoughtleaders are made or born, is the same true of acquiring a selling skill set?

Jim Masciarelli says yes. In his book *PowerSkills: Building Top-Level Relationships for Bottom-Line Results*, Jim gives selling the label "hunting" and almost eerily echoes Charles Garfield. "The good news is that 'hunting,' no matter how strongly affected by innate talent or cultural conditioning, can be learned," he writes.

> *Some of the most outstanding business leaders have admitted to me that hunting did not come naturally to them, that they had to learn it, and that once they did, its value in their professional lives proved enormous. Hunters, including the most successful ones, are by and large made, not born, and this raises hope for us all.*

A willingness to learn about how to become great at sales is therefore critical to successful implementation of your expert's edge, no matter what your product, service, job, or thoughtleading accomplishments. Even if you are a manager or other staff employee who might not think it's necessary to pay much attention to selling skills, you would do well to think again.

Are you in human resources, for example, seemingly far away from the sales department and all who live and breathe there? Or maybe you dwell in the fun, creative quarters of the marketing department, where leads are developed for the sales department, which then picks up the ball. Maybe your world is the numbers-only area of book-keeping or finance, or the quiet, solitary research and development division. Surely none of these functions need to know much, if anything, about sales.

Think again. Whenever you present your latest report or departmental results to your superiors, you are "selling" something. The form in which you cast your decisions and numbers needs to be interpreted. Conclusions must be drawn, and insights developed. New decisions will rest upon these insights, including continued or increased funding for your department. New projects will be decided upon and assigned. You are not a neutral player in such decisions. How you "sell" your point of view at such moments frequently determines what these decisions will be.

Actual Selling

Once you've vaulted the hurdle of your sales self-image and recognized the criticalness of developing yourself into what Jim Masciarelli calls a hunter, you need to learn all you can about selling skills so that you can leverage your thoughtleading actions for maximum success. The first principle to comprehend is what Alan Weiss calls "value distance," that is, demonstrating the most profound need possible—moving the value you offer away from a prospect's mere "want" of what you provide and closer and closer (decreasing the distance) to a raging "need" for that value. The more valuable you are perceived to be, Weiss explains, the more your prospect *must* have you, which also allows you to charge more because the potential ROI you have created is now dramatically higher.

Of course, Weiss is also famous for coining the phrase "get them to call you." This transformative result of a thoughtleading strategy can upend many standard selling assumptions, particularly the high levels of resistance present during most sales calls. When prospects call you rather than you calling them, they are three-quarters or more of the way there. They have already awarded you a deep vote of confidence and credibility that you otherwise would have had to earn as you struggled to convince them that they should even bother to talk to you. When prospects call you, they are often willing and eager to let you lead them. They expect that the call will go well, and they expect that they made the right choice by calling you. All you have to do is what our smart plumber did: be pleasant, knowledgeable, flexible, and accommodating. Confirm for your willing prospect that you are indeed an expert who can help sort things out and provide the desired service—just as the prospect assumed when placing the call.

Thought Notes

Do *Not* Try to Close Your Prospect, in Person or Ever

Of course, at some point you may have to say, "Well, should we do business together?" But is there anything better than a prospect who says, "OK, I'm sold. What's the next step?"

Sales Basics

Your thoughtleading actions should help you create this value distance and get them to call you, but it is your understanding of sales basics that will finish the process. Have you taken any time to acquire such an understanding? Most of us have to be pushed to do so, but once we have done this, the essentials we learn keep paying off in the form of business development results for years to come.

When I founded my previous business, CareerScape, I doubted my own sales ability and decided that I should do something to change that. My actual work as a CareerScape trainer and coach seemed pretty far removed from selling, but it did occur to me that if I didn't learn how to sell, I wouldn't be able to capture enough business to keep my new company viable.

So I joined an organization called Sales & Marketing Executives, even though I didn't think of myself as a sales or even a marketing executive by any means. I felt that by attending the group's breakfast seminars and networking sessions, I would soak up all kinds of tips and techniques for good selling, and that by rubbing shoulders with accomplished sales professionals, I'd also learn how smart sales pros thought, spoke, and acted.

I got involved in the organization too, volunteering to help with its programs and its newsletter. This brought me even closer to the basics of effective selling, as I interviewed experienced stars of the profession and listened to their presentations. I read books, too, during this period and took a few courses and seminars. After a year or so, I really began to feel I was getting the hang of it, not least because I was simply feeling confident and competent in my own execution of sales skills. I stopped viewing myself as clueless about how to turn my prospects into customers. My percentage of successful sales calls increased, transforming my overall professional self-image. The following are key lessons I learned for selling with success.

THOUGHT NOTES

The Five Gates of Selling

When push comes to shove in the selling cycle, it helps to know what you are doing. Sales success thoughtleader Duane Cashin adds that when you recognize that you must pass through five "gates" before you can close any sale, your selling skills will experience a major leap ahead. Here is how Duane explains this in an article he published in *Sales & Service Excellence* magazine:

As more and more companies leverage technology to copy their competitors' distinguishing advantages, more and more brands are starting to look alike. This makes it increasingly difficult for entrepreneurs to differentiate themselves for sales success. Yet this must be done! By passing through five "gates" during the process, you can beat this "brand-blur" syndrome and start winning, and keeping, new customers.

Gate #1: Likeability

People are more likely to buy from those they like. The more your prospect is genuinely interested in your product, and in you, the greater the likelihood that you will be liked. This is most important in the beginning stages as you only get to make one first impression. To establish Likeability:

- *Smile. Smiling sends many positive and inviting messages.*
- *Be "in the moment." When we are preoccupied or distracted, our prospect will not feel comfortable with us.*
- *Look your prospect in the eye.*
- *Ask relevant questions, then listen to the answers without interrupting.*
- *Provide feedback. This shows you have not only listened to your prospect's concerns but that you understand them as well and their importance.*

Gate #2: Credibility

A credible individual exhibits experience and knowledge ("credentials") relevant to the prospect's situation. Establish credibility prior to meeting with your prospect. To establish Credibility:

- *Explain business achievements and experiences related to your established success in delivering your product or services.*
- *Share relevant education. Being in touch with marketplace and industry changes shows you are up-to-date with the latest developments.*
- *Offer articles written by yourself. Every Revenue Generating Professional® should publish articles (like this one) commenting on issues in the marketplace.*
- *Offer letters of testimony. A most powerful way to establish credibility is with endorsements from satisfied customers/clients of the good work you have done.*

Gate #3: Respect

By respecting your prospects, you insure that you truly listen to their ideas. In turn, the level of respect you receive from your prospect increases each time you successfully fulfill a promise.

After establishing credibility, a prospect typically agrees to meet and share information on both a personal and professional level. This is called a "needs analysis." We gather meaningful information to the degree to which we have established Likeability, Credibility, and Respect. To establish Respect:

- *Before and after meeting with your prospect, offer articles relevant to their vertical market or industry, then be sure you really send them!*
- *Prior to your needs analysis meeting, send your prospect an agenda that gives an idea of the items you intend to cover.*
- *Show up for the needs analysis meeting early and avoid lengthy small talk.*

- *Prepare business questions for your needs analysis meeting, listening intently to the answers. Avoid interrupting! Interrupting rapidly erodes Likeability, Credibility, and Respect.*
- *Before answering a question or making a suggestion, always feed back what you understood your prospect to say.*
- *Never speak negatively about the competition. Take the position they are "good" professionals but that your solutions have proven to be "superior."*
- *After completing your needs analysis meeting, briefly summarize the prominent points you obtained from your prospect.*

Gate #4: Trust

When you demonstrate thoughtful consistency and when you deliver on your promises, you earn Trust. Assure your prospect that you have created a document full of references specifically designed to fit your prospect's needs. To establish Trust:

- *At the end of your needs analysis meeting, do a comprehensive recap. Hit as many relevant points as you can.*
- *Return with a customized proposal containing the prospect's language and concerns. By doing this, you'll continue to differentiate yourself from your competition.*
- *Explain how you went about creating your proposal.*
- *Be honest as you point out areas where your proposal might not be as strong as others'.*
- *Provide, as part of your proposal, documented testimonials, case studies and references. Back your claims up with evidence.*

Gate #5: Belief

Having moved through the Gates 1–4, Belief will be achieved. Upon passing through this final gate, your prospect will transform magically into a new customer. You will now understand exactly what to do to close new business prospects every time . . . and so you will!

Questions Are Critical

To succeed in your selling, asking questions is critical. Too often even sales reps fail because they just haven't learned to stop talking and start listening. They want so much to tell a prospect everything they can possibly think of about their fabulous product or service that they refuse to let their prospect get a word in edgewise. Most of the time, this is a fatal mistake.

The objective of basic sales questions is to identify what your prospect actually wants. This may not at all be the super-duper bells and whistles that you have decided are your product or service's greatest attraction. Start by asking the simplest question of them all: "What can I do for you?" Then pipe down and listen closely to what your prospect says. Keep asking more questions so that you acquire a deeper and deeper feel for what your prospect is seeking. Once you've heard enough, you can explain those aspects of your product or service that can help the prospect. By employing this method, you will not have to discuss those features, benefits, bells, or whistles that your prospect has not expressed interest in. You will be saving both of you lots of time and wasted breath.

If you ask questions and listen more, you can take a sales conversation to a higher level than either you or your prospect ever expected. If you can point out possible needs that the prospect hadn't considered, because you have listened closely to your prospect's perceived needs, you will be on the road to establishing value distance, positioning yourself not only as an expert who can solve problems but as an expert with an edge who can in fact add even greater value than your prospect could ever have imagined. Your prospect will soon begin believing that he or she would be a complete fool if he or she did not hire you. Once a prospect reaches this point, the next step is merely to iron out the details.

Questions to Ask Yourself

Along with questions to ask your prospects, there are a number of valuable questions that you should ask yourself about how you are going about the overall process. If you address these questions and adopt any new processes that the answers imply, your selling skills can take yet another great leap forward toward hunting proficiency.

1. Are You Targeting the Right Market?

When sales seem hard to come by, we often incorrectly identify our poor sales skills as the culprit. No one seems to be buying from me, we lament. Yet it may instead be that the market we've targeted just doesn't really and truly need our service. Or maybe it doesn't have the where-withal to afford our fees. My CareerScape services, for example, although obviously of tremendous potential benefit to out-of-work professionals, could not overcome the hurdle of that seemingly obvious target market's hesitation to spend any of its discretionary money, even for a worthwhile investment.

Could I have surmounted this hurdle by somehow shortening the value distance from my jobless prospects, somehow convincing them that my service would be not merely useful but essential? Possibly, but since the ratio of prospects to clients proved much higher, and far easier to achieve, with a new target market of *employed* professionals who were forward-looking enough to recognize the value of my program, it quickly proved far more profitable and less exhausting to set my sights on these targets and let the unemployed market fade away.

2. Are You Ranking Your Prospects?

Even when you are directing your efforts toward the right target prospects, certain categories of these prospects will tend to naturally become clients, whereas others will be difficult to sell no matter what. To keep yourself from running around and meeting with every prospect who comes floating your way, regardless of that prospect's potential to become your next client, try "ranking" your prospects according to their probability of becoming clients.

Do this by making up a list of characteristics of those who typically do hire you. Award weighted points for each of these characteristics. Also put on the list the characteristics of those who tend *not* to hire you. Weight these negative points as well. You'll end up with a scoring grid that you can divide into categories: High Probability, Moderately Probable, Ambiguous, Poor Prospect, Totally Unlikely.

For example, consultants tend to be the best prospects for me because they are entrepreneurs whose success depends upon their ideas and their intellectual judgment. They thus quickly see the value of publishing their ideas and attaining an "expert's edge." They also typically earn sufficient dollars to be able to afford me. They earn 3 points on my prospect ranking scale.

However, academics (professors, instructors, and teaching assistants), who would seemingly fall into the same category, rate a score of minus 4. Though they too recognize the value of getting published, they may feel limited by their fixed (and often somewhat paltry) salaries. An inquiry from an academic, then, no matter how successful that academic may be, is likely to result only in a "Well, let me think about it," rather than a new client thoughtleader. This despite the reality that some of the biggest thoughtleaders in the world are in fact academics, for example, Michael Porter, John Kotter, and Rosabeth Moss Kanter.

3. *Are You Making It* Too Easy *for a Prospect to Become Your Client?*

This may sound astonishingly counterintuitive, but in my experience, making your prospects jump through a few hoops before they sign on with you can be quite effective for weeding out the window-shoppers and tire kickers. Except in the early days of your business, when any kind of selling experience can be deemed "good practice," there eventually comes a time when you need to decide case by case who is worthy of your time. You can literally blow away every one of your business days by spending endless hours meeting and greeting folks who have merely expressed mild interest in your services. They come to you bearing such phrases as "I'd love to learn more about your services" and "Maybe we can meet and I can tell you about a project I have in mind."

But how serious are they?

Your ranking system can help with this, although sometimes, despite this nifty device, you can still get fooled.

Your protection against such time-wasting dangers is to stretch out your selling process a bit. Your aim here is to make your prospects jump through a series of hoops, so as to test their motivation.

"Tell me about your goals and how I can help you," is one good way to begin, rather than automatically accepting their invitation to run over to their place and meet. After they respond to that one (and *if* they respond to that one!), you can next let them know that they might want to read through a few specific pages on your Web site (a published article of yours, perhaps) in order to better understand the actual service they are asking about. Should a prospect not bother to read the suggested article and report back to you, then you have definitely dodged a bullet. If he won't even do that, the chances that he would have ponied up your fee down the road are slim. Plug this prospect's e-mail address into your e-list and forget him.

Note: If you're wondering why you would want to retain a weak prospect's e-mail address, then you weren't paying attention when we discussed the concept of your client community. Sometime in the future, today's poorly motivated prospect could evolve into a highly motivated one. Maybe this person's situation will get more urgent, thus decreasing your value distance. Or maybe the person will pass your name on to someone whose urgent need is already present. Unless you have an extremely good reason for keeping people off your e-list (such as an unscrupulous person or someone you absolutely cannot stand), then get everyone on there.

4. *Are You Presenting Yourself to Your Prospects as Their Equals?*

What distinguishes a thoughtleader from just another vendor is that a thoughtleader is truly the expert above all other experts. As a thoughtleader, you're the best there is; you're the go-to authority; you're the One Who Knows. Consequently, treat your prospect meeting as if you're already on the payroll. Listen, ask questions, explore, share, brainstorm helpful advice. As your prospect's thoughtleader (at that moment, anyway), walk in with an air of confidence that suggests that hiring you would never be a mistake. In fact, it could be one of the best decisions this prospect has made in a long, long time.

Alan Weiss puts it this way:

> *It's entirely within our power to control the sales process. But that requires the confidence to believe that you have value to offer and the diagnostic skills to determine what the actual issues are. Too often we act as order takers, obsequious beggars with our hat in our hand, hoping we'll be chosen. We should, of course, position ourselves as independent and objective experts, peers of the buyer, who can provide ideas, provocation, and new perspectives on the spot.*

5. Do You Assume that a "No-Sale" Prospect Meeting Means You Blew It?

A meeting with a sales prospect is often just that: a meeting. You do not have to walk out with a sale; you do not have to view it as your "only shot." In fact, the best next step may be to put together a requested proposal or even to come back for a second meeting, this time with more of the prospect's decision makers involved. Purposely stretching out the sales process is always a good thing, since a rush to close a sale often indicates insufficient due diligence, resulting in a client relationship that never should have existed. Such clients turn into the proverbial clients from hell, always wondering if they made the right decision when they hired you, looking over your shoulder to see if their ROI is truly coming in, second-guessing you, and sometimes taking their sweet old time to pay you.

So stretch it out. Test and build this new relationship, send thank-you notes, send a copy of your book, ask for more materials to help you compose your proposal, send an e-mail link to one of your recent media appearances. Keep the relationship building. Don't overdo it, though. There's a fine line between stretching the process out and making it interminably annoying. Experiment to discover where your particular fine line falls. Then keep dancing toward it, just enough to allow both you and your prospect to determine if you've got the right fit.

Thought Notes

Leave Fees *Out* of the First Draft of Your Proposal

By sending a preliminary proposal covering everything *except* fees, you can both further the relationship-building effort of this maverick selling approach and be absolutely certain that you understand what your prospect wants from you. Keep submitting your proposal without fees until you've nailed down exactly what your prospect is looking for.

Turning Speaking Gigs into Sales

Do you perceive your speaking engagements as one-time opportunities? You've got one chance to get in front of a throng of potential buyers and make your pitch, right? Then you go home and hope that something happens.

If you behave this way, join the crowd! It's a passive approach, much like most folks' handling of their published articles, and it's not worthy of a thoughtleader or an expert with an edge.

To maximize your speaking opportunities, integrate them into your overall thoughtleading business strategy. This means implementing the following thoughtleading actions.

1. *Distribute Your Published Article(s) as Handouts.*
Don't leave your published articles at home, particularly if you have an article that covers precisely the same topic as your presentation. Print up nice glossy versions of your article, ask your meeting planner in advance how many attendees are expected, then try to get your hand-outs distributed to every table or chair before you begin speaking.

Bring along stacks of copies of your other published articles as well, in case there's an information table set up somewhere where you can leave these articles, as well as copies of your brochure and even your business cards. You never know if such a table will be set up, so always be ready, just in case.

2. *Bring Your Book for Sale.*
If you've published a book, bring copies for sale. Ask your meeting planner if he or she can recruit someone to sell the book for you in the back of the room; if not, ask for a guest pass so that you can bring your own assistant to do this. For book sales success, base your presentation on your book's central topic, or at least find ways to relate your topic to portions of the book. Keep holding up the book as you mention it, as this reminds your listeners that if they want to bring you home, your book is the way to do so.

Some speaker-authors like to give a book or two away before or during their talk, maybe for answering a pop-quiz question. This helps place your book right in the midst of your audience. The visual picture of someone nearby holding (and owning) your book will whet some attendees' appetites for owning a copy themselves.

3. *Collect Those Business Cards!*
As your audience's thoughtleader-of-the-moment, act as though you in fact really do care about keeping up your newfound relationships. Go around saying hello to folks before you get up to speak, exchanging business cards and offering a copy of your published article or even your book.

You might also pass around a basket or hat as you begin your talk, requesting everyone's business card and explaining exactly why you want them: "I plan to keep in touch with all of you after this talk by putting you on my e-list. You can always unsubscribe, of course, but I believe we all must find ways to build relationships with one another and keep them going. I'll put you on my e-list, and I want you to put me on yours. That way, we'll stay in touch and grow both our networks." Speak the truth here; don't engage in phony games like raffling off your book or a fruit basket just so you can collect cards. Let the chips fall where they may and you'll be surprised at how many of them fall squarely at your feet.

4. *Thank Everyone the Next Day.*
Another relationship mistake common to all too many public speakers is their practice of completely ignoring all these new relationships the very next day, even if they have in fact collected many business cards. Do not do this!

The very next morning, without fail, you or your assistant must input all this juicy new contact information into your database, then send out a thank-you e-mail to every attendee who let you have his or her card. Your message should be something simple, like this:

Hello Joe!

Thank you so much for coming out and listening to me at the Business Circle event yesterday. I do hope my presentation was worthwhile. As promised, I am putting you on my e-list, and I hope that you will put me on yours as well. By all means, let's stay in touch. Perhaps I'll see you at another Business Circle event sometime soon.

Regards,

Ken Lizotte

Such a short-but-sweet e-mail thank-you goes a long way toward advancing whatever connection you made the day before, even if you never actually met Joe. Now Joe is willing to receive your e-blasts, which will allow you to communicate with him indefinitely. The beginning of a beautiful relationship!

Only one note of caution here: if you are a provider of professional services, do not betray Joe's trust by battering him with blatant advertisements. He has come to know you as a thoughtleader, so act like one. Send Joe useful information, news, your published articles, or tips. Promote yourself and your firm in the same indirect way you do when you are speaking: by offering useful ideas. Don't suddenly bait and switch and open the advertising floodgates. If you do, Joe will justifiably unsubscribe so fast it'll make your laptop spin. Plus, he'll spread very bad word of mouth about you, the kind that will undo all the good you have worked so hard to attain.

However, as I mentioned in a previous chpater, there is an exception to this rule: if your business is product-centered or one focused more on your service than on yourself (such as catering, package delivery, a dress shop, or corporate gift boxes), it might be OK to send out direct advertising e-mails. Your presentation will have prepared the members of your audience for this kind of product information, and so they'll be more likely to accept even the most shameless advertising plugs. In fact, they'll *want* to hear about a discount or a sale or a new product that's available. Only in this case are straightforward e-commercials A-OK.

These kinds of follow-ups alone will distinguish you from your competitors, cementing your prospects' view that you stand alone as the true expert here. Also, you are someone whom they are beginning to know, someone who apparently actually cares about building a relationship with them. Consciously or subconsciously, their sensing that will separate you from the pack.

14

How Thoughtleading
Serves Us All

What you get by achieving your goals is not as important as what you become by achieving your goals.

ZIG ZIGLAR

ADOPTING THOUGHTLEADING as a business strategy will equip you and your business with the expert's edge, advancing you far beyond your competition and keeping you there. By heeding what I've had to say in these pages, you'll place yourself within a very different business reality, maintaining high levels of proficiency and expertise, attracting qualified prospects who come to you on a regular basis seemingly out of nowhere, eliminating boom-and-bust cycles, and establishing yourself as a unique authority that both your target market and the media automatically turn to every time. A song from the fifties by the Platters, "Only You," will sound like it was written with you in mind.

From here on, your new prospects will view you as an expert who stands head and shoulders above all the rest. They will often show no interest in even considering anyone else—no interviews with other candidates, no requests to see references, and in some cases even no need for a formal business proposal. They will simply want to do business with you before they even meet you: "only you and you alone," as the song goes.

As they come your way, however, your prospects will be anxious about one thing that is gnawing at them: can they afford you? For some, your fees will be a major stretch, yet they will dig down deeper and somehow come up with the money. Where else, after all, can they go? Where else, after all, would they *want* to go? *You* are the thoughtleader, *you* are the go-to-authority—"only you and you alone."

Such outstanding business development results surely offer enough to justify your heading down this very different path, yet you know by now that thoughtleading also offers much more. A pure passion for your business, for example, will unfold within you, deepening your enjoyment of it and expanding your self-confidence as its leader. No longer either just a job or your master, your chosen focus will continually renew itself, staying vital, surprising, and energized. Kudos will regularly come your way in appreciation of the enlightening knowledge and advice that you transmit daily, whether to clients, prospects, readers, audiences, media, or colleagues.

The impact of your personal passion for what you do will expand as well. An old adage among motivational experts asserts that "preference breeds expertise." By loving what you do more deeply, you will get better and better at it, and your customers will notice. Whether you are a management consultant or an IP attorney or an engineer or a product manufacturer, you will elevate the value of your knowledge and skill again and again and again as you strive to be the best at what you do. Your contributions to your specialty will never rest. For a thoughtleader, there is always opportunity, and desire, to improve yet again and to keep leaping forward.

Has Harvey Mackay's thoughtleading contributed to the day-to-day operations of his envelope manufacturing company?

Of course. By developing his thoughtleading ideas focused on extraordinary customer service, Harvey has continually transformed the way his envelope company serves its customers. Before long, you too will notice how your thoughtleading ideas have infused your overall business, not just by increasing your revenue stream but by raising the bar for your service or product in a manner you could not previously have imagined.

And it won't stop there. Within your new context of constantly bettering your service to customers, your thoughtleading will create repercussions that, lofty as this sounds, can contribute to a better world. Your ethics will start showing up on your own radar screen. They will no longer be annoying blips that are passed over in the bustle of each frantic day. Instead, they will now take center stage, because your thoughtleading mindset will no longer allow you to pull punches or just slip by. The services you provide will henceforth be performed to the absolute best of your ability as your thoughtleading deepens your commitment to getting things done right for your clients, that is, fairly, impeccably, and accountably.

Many of The Donald's writings indicate this, containing passages in which he reflects on ethically ambiguous business episodes which, if not for the need to analyze them in a book, might have zipped through his consciousness without his giving them another thought. Like many high-wheeling dealmakers, he might never have a good reason to slow down and pick apart the moral implications of his decisions or his process for making them.

Michael Shenkman, author of *Leader Mentoring* and *The Arch and the Path: The Life of Leading Greatly* explains it this way:

> *I completely trust that no one sets out to be an unethical thoughtleader. However, one can easily mistake one's own opinions, ideologies, or beliefs for being "leading" thoughts. Taking responsibility for thoughtleading also means doing the work—the research, the field testing, engaging in an open contest of ideas—in order to be sure that what is being proffered as a "leading" thought actually is one.*

Then one has to be willing to make the investment in time that it takes to put the thought out there, have it be heard, and occasionally understood. The idea of getting quick fame and fortune from being a thoughtleader is a pipe dream. What you get is the opportunity to do the work that means the most to you, representing it and putting it to work in the world. The joy in it all is that you get to live what you believe, and see it play out in action.

Jay Vogt, founder of Peoplesworth, expresses similar sentiments about how the practice of thoughtleading affects his moral compass and that of his consulting and training firm and its clients. Jay's firm helps people who lead organizations "discover greater creativity, spirit, and harmony in their workplaces," a mission that leads him to write and publish books and articles on subjects like "grounded" visioning, community building, and "unpredictable ways to release the natural intelligence of your organization." Thoughtleading efforts, he says, afford him "a great opportunity to express myself, while offering concepts and tools that are of real value to my clients. Over time my published ideas have become a body of work that catalogs tangible ways my clients can become both better companies and better people."

Some organizations attempt to help individual business experts with this struggle to maintain a high-level commitment to accountability and ethics, and keep such values on the front burner. Mark Haas, National Board Chair of the Institute of Management Consultants USA (IMC USA), the professional association and certifying body for management consultants in the United States, cites ethics as the foundation of an effective consultant. IMC USA's CMC, or Certified Management Consultant, for example, not only evaluates a consultant's experience, client satisfaction, and consulting competence, but also requires that CMC candidates demonstrate strong ethics via both written and oral ethics examinations, a rigorous Code of Ethics, and submission to a clear enforcement process. This is something true thoughtleaders would likely jump at so as to publicly display that aspect of their Expert's Edge. Haas explains it this way:

The CMC represents more than just disciplinary skill or industry experience possessed by many business advisors. It signifies exceptional commitment to maintaining their consulting businesses and delivering consulting services with a deliberately high-level consulting competence and professional behaviors based on an international consulting competency framework and body of knowledge. Most consultants aren't even aware of these competencies while CMCs continuously develop and bring the full range of them to each client assignment and prove repeatedly their commitment to consulting as a profession.

The CMC is also grounded in detailed ethics requirements, also unusual among consultants, the stereotypes of whom are often used as examples of bad ethics or sleazy business practices. A CMC has had to pass both written and oral ethics examinations, ascribe to a strong Code of Ethics, voluntarily submit to rigorous compliance procedures, and regularly get ethics training. Clients are best served when their management advisors are proven, trusted and reliable business partners who both know how to do things right as well as can be trusted to do the right thing. In each of the 44 countries where it is awarded, the CMC signifies a higher standard of value that the consultant possessing one offers to a client.

Your "Thought Following"

Finally, the more you base your business actions upon passion, excellence, and ethics, the more your behavior begins to literally inspire others, spreading your good thoughts and deeds out the way a smooth stone thrown into a pond sends ripples across the water symmetrically in every direction for as far as your eye can see. Thoughtleading has the word *leading* in it for a reason: You will literally lead the way, as Alan Weiss has said, for others to follow, not just for your business offerings, but to follow your example as well.

As you delve deeply into your work, your "thought followers" will recognize that yours is the proper, effective, and meaningful way to go. You'll inspire your followers to similarly commit themselves to an all-out goal of upgrading themselves as experts, as entrepreneurs, as business owners, as professionals—and, yes, as better people too. You'll inspire them to work not merely to get by or to collect a paycheck, but to fully realize themselves as they strive to contribute what matters.

Thus, by creating a thought following, you will lead others to pursue their own passions and develop their own leading thoughts. They will deliver outstanding professional services, manufacture excellent new products, improve the quality of their goods and services as a matter of course, care about their customer service, and streamline their processes—all because of what they have seen in *you*. The ripple effect of what you do will extend far and wide.

So while most of this book has spotlighted thoughtleading as an extraordinary business development strategy, our final note embraces its capacity to transform individuals beyond themselves on a personal scale. Through the ages, thoughtleading has afforded humanity both gifts and evil. In the twentieth century, we saw the brave sunlight of FDR and Churchill on one side and the dark horror of Hitler and Stalin on the other. In the nineteenth century, Abraham Lincoln and Frederick Douglass and Susan B. Anthony held high the lamp of freedom, while slave owners and patriarchal power structures fought tooth and nail—even literally to the death—to keep their bonds tight and permanent. In the seventeenth century, colonists advocating a strange new governance concept called "democracy," something that was quite unheard of, stood ragged but strong against a monarchal world empire, centuries old in its assumed moral legitimacy. We can go on and on with our stark historical examples, and if we peer into our personal business lives, we can often find the same. So within such comparative spectrums, the question to face is: where do I fall?

Thoughtleading can provide your personal answer. As a yardstick by which to measure every judgment, every decision, and every ultimate action, thoughtleading affords an operating principle to guide you toward your personal best.

"Where do I fall?" It's certainly one way to phrase the question, although a better way might be: "Where do I rise?" By committing yourself to the practice of thoughtleading, you will continually rise, continually pull yourself up, and continually push on for the top. And by merely attempting this, you will win.

By merely attempting, you install yourself as the go-to authority, on a plane significantly above much, or all, of your competition. Your trying alone begins getting you there because your competitors, for the most part, will never strive for, let alone achieve, even this much. In the final analysis, it's not just that you know a lot about something or that you know more than anyone else, but that your thoughtleading demonstrates how very much you care.

That, in the end, wins the ballgame.

Afterthoughts

WITHIN THE FORMAT OF ANY BOOK, many great thoughts, ideas, opinions, and clever remarks that the author wished to include just don't fit, for a variety of reasons. Perhaps the point has been made with another quote or paragraph, or perhaps the message, while insightful or witty, falls a tad outside the focus of the chapter or of the book itself. But rather than throw away all these choice nuggets, I decided to include them here, at the end, in a potpourri labeled "Afterthoughts." Enjoy them with a snifter of brandy or a fine Cuban cigar.

Ralph Waldo Emerson
What is the hardest task in the world? To think!

Francis Moore Lappe
The only real risk is the risk of thinking too small.

Alan Weiss

If you're not publishing, if you're not speaking, if you're not sought out by others, then you're not a thoughtleader. If you feel you can't do those things, you need to content yourself with *not* being a thoughtleader.

Carl Friesen

Author of *The Fame Game* (SMPS)

Understanding what a guru is and does will give you a pretty good idea of whether you want to become one. Consider these benefits:

- *Choice of work.* Because of the star power and marquee value a guru has, you can choose which assignments to take, when, and for how long. You also have the rare privilege of "firing" a client if you want. Anyone can do this, of course, but for non-gurus the consequences may be more severe.
- *More money.* Generally, an acknowledged guru is able to bill at multiples of the rate charged for a garden-variety professional. This means that you can either earn more per year or spend more time on other worthy pursuits. Depending on your circumstances, this might include attending your child's T-ball game, perfecting that golf swing, or climbing the highest peaks on all seven continents.
- *Popularity.* People will pick up the check at lunch, buy you drinks, and laugh at your jokes . . . even when they're awful.

Francis Bacon

A wise man will make more opportunities than he finds.

William Jennings Bryan

Destiny is no matter of chance, it is a matter of choice. It is not a thing to be waited for . . . it is a thing to be achieved.

Tom Schinkel
Founder, Thomas Schinkel Associates

When you try to present an objective perspective or a thoughtleading perspective, you need to have patience to allow people to come around to your point of view. Sometimes the noise level is very high because of euphoria, and sometimes people are in a doom-and-gloom stage. In either case, you need to work with them. It takes patience.

Thomas A. Edison

The first requisite for success is the ability to apply your physical and mental energies to one problem incessantly without growing weary.

Peter Drucker

When you are the chief executive, you're the prisoner of your organization. The moment you're in the office, everybody comes to you and wants something, and it is useless to lock the door. They'll break in. So, you have to get outside the office. But still, that isn't traveling. That's being at home or having a secret office elsewhere. When you're alone, in your secret office, ask the question, "What needs to be done?" Develop your priorities and don't have more than two. I don't know anybody who can do three things at the same time and do them well. Do one task at a time or two tasks at a time. That's it. OK, two works better for most. Most people need the change of pace. But, when you are finished with two jobs or reach the point where it's futile, make the list again. Don't go back to priority three. At that point, it's obsolete.

Harry Lauder

The future is not a gift—it is an achievement.

William James

He who refuses to embrace a unique opportunity loses the prize as surely as if he had failed.

Patricia Coate

West Coast Manager, emerson consulting group

Because you will have control over the expression of your ideas, writing bylined articles is a much better "first step" (and second and third step) on your way to publicity and fame than waiting for journalists and editors to call you for an interview. If you do that, you'll never know how it'll come out.

Peter Drucker

Successful leaders don't start out asking, "What do I want to do?" They ask, "What needs to be done?" Then they ask, "Of those things that would make a difference, which are right for me?" They don't tackle things they aren't good at. They make sure other necessities get done, but not by them. Successful leaders make sure that they succeed! They are not afraid of strength in others. Andrew Carnegie wanted to put on his gravestone, "Here lies a man who knew how to put into his service more able men than he was himself."

Emily Dickinson

Dwell on possibilities.

Yogi Berra

Ninety percent of the game is half mental.

Alan Weiss

Steven Leavitt, author of *Freakonomics*, just knew he had to popularize what he was saying. He didn't want to just teach his students at Stanford; he said, "I've got to get a book out."

Jeff Govendo

President, The Innovative Edge

There is an all-too-common complaint heard from participants after a creativity retreat is over: "It was great while we were out there, but as soon as we got back to work, we immediately settled into our old routines." And since these tend to be the very routines that the outing was supposed to shake up a bit, one could argue that despite the participants' having had a good time, from an ROI perspective the outing wasn't worth the time or money.

What is missing in many of these corporate outings is the additional, critical step of processing, or debriefing, the experience the participants just went through. When this processing step is glossed over or omitted entirely, it's much less likely that the gains will show up in any meaningful way back at the workplace. The experience is remembered as something that was fun and exciting, but that had little connection to everyday work life.

Alan Weiss

I always say that if you don't blow your own horn, you can't hear the music. True thoughtleaders don't just sit back and let people read their works; they get out and promote them, talk about them.

Amanda Miller
Meeting Planner

Publishing an article is a formidable and potentially rewarding marketing activity, yet all too many successful article authors fail to participate much, or at all, in the process during the period *after* publication. Consequently, they end up missing out on their article's most powerful benefits. Here are five common mistakes:

> Mistake 1. Hiding away your published article in a filing cabinet
> Mistake 2. Not informing your clients, prospects, and colleagues of your published article
> Mistake 3. Forgetting to post your article on your company's Web site
> Mistake 4. Not bothering to add your article to your marketing kit, or mention it in your CV or company brochure
> Mistake 5. Failing to use your new relationship with a publication editor to propose and publish future articles

Steve Markman

President, Markman Speaker Management

When you speak, create high-impact presentations! Audiences want to acquire actionable information they can take back to their companies. A solid, informative presentation that is purely educational in nature and is not product or service or company-specific will create instant credibility for the speaker and the information provided. In contrast, a sales pitch is not only unnecessary, but harmful. A presentation that turns out to be a sales pitch insures the "kiss of death," including low evaluations from your audience.

Alan Weiss

As for speaking, some common mistakes are being too conceptual or giving away the store. You should be whetting people's appetite. And a thoughtleader always provokes. Most speakers stand up there and want to be loved; I stand up there and want to be hired. They want high scores from five out of five; I need only one.

Peter Drucker

The value of the Internet? Let me give you one example. This happens to be a consulting firm headquartered in Boston. Each morning, between 8 a.m. and 9 a.m. Boston time, which is 5 a.m. in the morning here in California and 11 p.m. in Tokyo, the firm conducts a one-hour management meeting on the Internet. That would have been inconceivable a few years back when you couldn't have done it physically. And for a few years, I worked with this firm closely and I had rented a room in a nearby motel and put in a videoconferencing screen. Once a week, I participated in this Internet meeting and we could do it quite easily, successfully. As a result of which, that consulting firm is not organized around localities but around clients.

Patricia Coate

West Coast Manager, emerson consulting group

The goal of any selling process should be the winning over of a truly partnership-minded client, one that will eagerly appreciate what you do.

Ralph Waldo Emerson

To know even one life has breathed easier because you have lived. This is to succeed.

Mohandas Gandhi

We must be the change we wish to see.

Index

About the Author

Ken Lizotte, CMC, Chief Imaginative Officer (CIO) of emerson consulting group inc. (www.thoughtleading.com), is a long-time thought-leader who has been interviewed or profiled by many media, including *BusinessWeek*, *Fortune*, *Newsweek*, *Writer's Digest*, *CBS News*, and *National Public Radio*.

Ken's consulting firm transforms companies, executives, professional service firms, solo consultants, attorneys, and law firms into thoughtleaders, separating them from their competition and lifting their businesses to new heights.

A former columnist for the American Management Association and a cofounder of the National Writers Union, Ken has authored four previous books and hundreds of published articles. He speaks regularly on such topics as becoming a thoughtleader, publishing books and articles, balancing work and family, personal creativity, and discovering your "dream career." An expert at leading interactive seminars, he has been facilitating business/career workshops at the Harvard University Extension School since 1995.

President of the New England chapter of IMC USA (the Institute of Management Consultants) from 2000 to 2005, he is a current member of IMC USA's national Board of Directors and has earned its prestigious "CMC" (Certified Management Consultant) credential, a mark that designates the highest standards of consulting professionalism and adherence to its ethical canons. Less than 1 percent of all consultants worldwide have achieved this enviable level of performance and certification.

Ken lives in Concord, Massachusetts, within jogging distance of the historic homes of Ralph Waldo Emerson and Louisa May Alcott, and a short amble from Henry David Thoreau's cabin at Walden Pond.